Laughter In The Dark

A Comedy

Victor Lucas

Samuel French - London
New York – Sydney – Toronto – Hollywood

© 1954 by Victor Lucas

This play is fully protected under the Copyright Laws of the British Commonwealth of Nations, the United States of America and all countries of the Berne and Universal Copyright Conventions.

All rights including Stage, Motion Picture, Radio, Television, Public Reading, and Translation into Foreign Languages, are strictly reserved.

No part of this publication may lawfully be reproduced in ANY form or by any means — photocopying, typescript, recording (including video-recording), manuscript, electronic, mechanical, or otherwise — or be transmitted or stored in a retrieval system, without prior permission.

Rights of Performance by Amateurs are controlled by Samuel French Ltd, 52 Fitzroy Street, London W1T 5JR, and they, or their authorized agents, issue licences to amateurs on payment of a fee. **It is an infringement of the Copyright to give any performance or public reading of the play before the fee has been paid and the licence issued.**

Licences are issued subject to the understanding that it shall be made clear in all advertising matter that the audience will witness an amateur performance; that the names of the authors of the plays shall be included on all announcements and all programmes; and that the integrity of the authors' work will be preserved.

The Royalty Fee indicated below is subject to contract and subject to variation at the sole discretion of Samuel French Ltd.

    Basic fee for each and every
        performance by amateurs   Code K
        in the British Isles

In Theatres or Halls seating Six Hundred or more the fee will be subject to negotiation.

In Territories Overseas the fee quoted above may not apply. A fee will be quoted on application to our local authorized agent, or if there is no such agent, on application to Samuel French Ltd, London.

The Professional Rights in this play are controlled by Samuel French Ltd, 52 Fitzroy Street, London W1T 5JR.

The publication of this play does not imply that it is necessarily available for performance by amateurs or professionals, either in the British Isles or Overseas. Amateurs and professionals considering a production are strongly advised in their own interests to apply to the appropriate agents for consent before starting rehearsals or booking a theatre or hall.

ISBN 978 0 573 11218 8

CHARACTERS

Gripe, a revolting butler, decrepit and decayed
Alathea Budgett, a good-looking and dominating woman of fifty
Herbert Budgett, her husband. Bald-headed, short-sighted and shy
Belinda Budgett, their daughter, sweet and shrewd
Cyril Carraway, an amiable and fatuous young man
Bunny Tucker, a likeable little blonde
Thundercloud, a very large Red Indian—with a Greek accent
Gosforth, a legal gentleman
Lydia Prentice, a sophisticated secretary—allergic to he-men
Alec Ogleby, hearty and expansive with a roving eye
Aunty Emily Budgett, a fierce little spinster with bright beady eyes
Several non-speaking Spectres

The action of the play takes place at Creeching Cheyney, a faded mansion in Hampshire

ACT I   Christmas Eve

ACT II   Scene 1   An hour later
           Scene 2   Later that night

ACT III   Christmas Day

PRODUCTION NOTES

The play requires zest and pace from all concerned, not forgetting Aunt Emily, whose particular responsibility it is to ensure that the tempo does not flag at the end.

Herbert and Bunny must be portrayed as real and likeable people, genuinely attracted to each other. Gripe can, of course, be played with especial relish. Beware of the danger of slowing him down to an "old man" pace which would cause him to drop the general tempo. Alec must be absolutely sure of himself. Much of the pace of the play depends on his breezy, confidence-inspiring, quick-talking performance. Thundercloud is also a very forceful character but must avoid over-riding Cyril's and Herbert's laughs.

The ghost's business in the drinking scene must not be laboured. The passing of the glasses should be done naturally and swiftly. The dialogue is timed to coincide with the ghost's moves and the directions in the script should be adhered to. Alec and Cyril cannot wait for extra business from the ghost nor should they remain unnaturally still while the ghost is on.

The door knocker should be large and heavy and the knocking equally so. The chain on the door must *not* be painted string and the bar should be of metal. As regards the chains which clank off stage . . . the heavier the better. The sliding panel can be masked behind by a large square of black cloth on the principle of a photographer's hood.

The ghost at the end of Act II, Scene Two is supposedly Gosforth in disguise but can be portrayed by another person of Gosforth's build, his features hidden by the mask.

Several pairs of hands will be needed back stage and may well belong to the actors appearing briefly as apparitions, but at the final curtain further assistance will be needed.

The glasses which Alec brings on in Act II, Scene Two should be dark in colour, so that Alec and Cyril are not obliged to empty their glasses each time in the interests of realism!

In Act II, Scene Two someone must be standing by off stage near the top of the stairs in readiness for Cyril's exit, to effect a lighting change over of bowler hats. A stage wait here would be disastrous. Have the names of the recipients clearly marked on each of the presents in Gripe's sack.

After Gripe enters to Aunt Emily, change gel to green in the flood outside the door DL and have it turned so that when the door opens the flood will shine across the stage on to the centre door. Ensure that there is no spill of light on to the stage before the door is opened.

The church bells must be muffled and distant. If hanging chimes are used instead of a record, the clock chime a few minutes later must have a different note and come from a different source. If possible have the church bells off left and the clock chime off right.

When the kitchen door opens of its own accord it is quite simply opened off by someone behind it, watching the ghost carefully through a small hole in the flat.

The twang of the bowstring can be supplied by plucking a fiddle string loudly.

The snapping and crackling as the fire is lit is best contrived by breaking up a piece of thin plywood with pliers behind the fireplace.

ACT I

Christmas Eve at Creeching Cheyney, a faded, eerie mansion in Hampshire

DL *is a door leading to the kitchen.* UL *is an archway entrance at the top of a flight of steps. At the top of the stairs is a small window. In the back wall, right of* C, *is a solid-looking main door. There is another door* UR, *below which is the fireplace.* R *of the main door is a large leaded window which starts about four feet above the floor*

The main items of furniture are a dining table L *with three chairs around it and a settee* UR. *There is a deep armchair* DL, *an umbrella stand-cum-coat rack* L *of the main door, a small telephone table* UL *and a cabinet for drinks above the kitchen door. In front of the fireplace is a long fire-stool. The furniture is solid and antique. At the start of the play most of it is shrouded by white sheets. There are sundry bookcases, stags' heads, crossed halberds etc.*

The main lighting is from wall-brackets controlled by a switch immediately R *of the main door. There is also a standard lamp above the fireplace*

As the CURTAIN *rises the stage is in darkness, pierced by a flash of lightning. Rain, thunder and gusts of wind can be heard*

There is a horrible peal of maniacal laughter off stage, followed by the rattling of heavy chains. There is a loud knocking at the door. More thunder. The knocking is repeated. A grotesque shadow appears on the wall as Gripe enters at the top of the stairs holding aloft a flickering lantern. Like the house, he is old and rambling

Gripe Did somebody knock?

The wind howls and is accompanied by a high-pitched moaning offstage

Or was it the wind that howls round these old walls? Howling! ... Howling! (*He throws back his head and howls*)

The knocking is heard again as the wind increases

Who's there? Can't you lie quiet in the earth, blast you!

Knocking again as Gripe unbars the door

All right, all right. I'm coming. (*He opens the door about a foot on a chain*) What do you want?
Alathea (*off*) Is this Creeching Cheyney?
Gripe It is. What do you want?
Alathea (*off*) We want to come in. We're getting soaked out here!
Herbert (*off*) Open the door! Open the door I say!

Gripe Who are you? What are you doing out at this time of night?
Alathea (*off*) I'm Mrs Budgett.
Herbert (*off*) And I'm Mr Budgett.
Gripe Who? Budgett? Never heard of you. Go away. (*He shuts the door*)

There is more knocking

(*Switching on lights and opening the door a little as before*) There's nobody here. Only me. Go away.
Alathea (*off*) We've come to live here.
Herbert (*off*) Yes, we've come to live here.
Gripe Nobody lives here. Nobody could. Nobody would.

The wind rises

Go away.
Alathea (*off*) Will you open this door!
Gripe Why?
Alathea (*off*) Because I tell you to! This house belongs to us.
Gripe No it don't. Belongs to Mr Cheyney.
Alathea (*off*) No it doesn't, it belongs to us. Mr Cheyney died and left the house to us.
Gripe What's that you say? Mr Cheyney dead? The master dead! Lord save us! Why didn't you say so before. (*He unbolts the chain and opens the door*) Standing out there nattering. Keeping me hanging about here in the draught . . .

Alathea and Herbert enter, their teeth chattering with cold, stamping their feet and blowing on frozen fingers. Herbert staggers under the weight of two large suitcases. Alathea is a good-looking but forbidding woman of fifty, tall and well-built. Herbert is a nice little man, bald-headed, short-sighted and shy. In his late forties

Gripe It'll be your fault if I catch my death of cold.
Alathea You horrible old man. What do you mean by shutting the door in my face! I suppose you're Gripe?
Gripe (*cupping his hand to his ear*) Eh? When?
Alathea Gripe! I said you must be Gripe!
Gripe Yes? Well I'm not surprised. And serve you right too.
Alathea Oh! I knew we should have waited until after Christmas.
Herbert But we couldn't, my dear. The terms of the will were most explicit.
Alathea I shall be glad when Cyril and Belinda get here. It will be a comfort to have a man about the place.
Herbert Yes, my dear.
Gripe (*tugging at Herbert's sleeve*) 'Ere! When did the master die, eh?
Alathea Mr Cheyney died last month and left us everything in his will. This house and all he possessed.
Gripe Left it all to you?
Alathea To my husband. Mr Cheyney was his Uncle Desmond.
Gripe He left you two all his money?
Alathea Yes.

Act I

Gripe Silly old fool.
Alathea I beg your pardon!
Gripe (*shaking her by the hand*) My name's Gripe. How do you do.
Alathea Are you the butler referred to in Mr Cheyney's will?
Gripe Eh? It will. Yes, it will.
Alathea This is insufferable! Herbert, why don't you make yourself useful instead of standing there shaking yourself like a wet dog.
Herbert I'm sorry my dear.
Alathea Take charge of this nasty old man and get him to light a fire while I see what the other rooms are like. (*Pointing* UR) Where does that door lead to?
Gripe Them was the master's private compartments.
Alathea (*switching on the standard lamp*) What's up those stairs?
Gripe Beds.
Alathea And how many servants are there?
Gripe None.
Alathea (*horrified*) Do you mean to say there's nobody else in the house!
Gripe That's right. Just you. (*He grins toothlessly*) And me.
Alathea This is dreadful. I can't think why your Uncle Desmond insisted we live here for a whole year. He must have had a warped sense of humour.

Alathea exits DL

Gripe 'Ere. (*He plucks at Herbert's sleeve*) 'Ere, tell me. Tell me, what did he die of? Was it ... was it—poison? Eh? How did you do it, eh? In his porridge?
Herbert Certainly not! I don't understand you. He died in Australia.
Gripe (*removing a dust sheet from the umbrella stand*) Oh, I see. That makes it a bit more difficult, don't it?
Herbert You'd better light a fire. You heard what she said.
Gripe Yes, all right. I don't mind. I'm a bit chilly myself. (*He crosses to the fire and kneels before it*) Now, come on, tell me all about it. (*Ominously*) You don't want to live here, you know.
Herbert Why shouldn't we?
Gripe (*pursing his lips*) Ooh, I wouldn't if I was you! Course it's different for me. I don't mind 'em. I'm used to 'em.
Herbert You're used to what?
Gripe (*conspiratorially*) I'll tell you. Come 'ere.

Herbert moves towards him, but Gripe suddenly changes his mind

No, I won't. Better not. You wouldn't like it.
Herbert What do you mean?
Gripe Nothing. (*He chuckles soundlessly*) Nothing at all. (*He strikes a match to light the fire*)

Alathea enters DL

Look out. Here she comes.
Alathea The kitchen is quite disgusting. There's a pile of dirty plates that must have been there for a month.

A snapping and crackling sound comes from the fire

(*To Gripe*) You must get a girl from the village tomorrow to clean the place up. I wouldn't trust you to do it yourself.
Gripe Can't get nobody tomorrow. It's Christmas Day. Anyway, they wouldn't come. Not Christmas, nor any other day.
Alathea Why not?
Gripe Aaah . . . !
Alathea I shall lose my patience in a moment. If the employer was anything like the servant, I'm grateful we never met your Uncle Desmond.

Alathea exits UL

Gripe What's this? You never met him? What did he leave you this house for then? There's something fishy about this.
Herbert Not at all. It was something of a surprise but I believe he was always rather eccentric.
Gripe I don't know about that, but he was always a wicked old scoundrel. Filled with all the sins of the flesh. (*He uncovers the armchair*) He was a proper devil for the women. Couldn't leave 'em alone. (*He cackles*) I could tell you things about what went on in this house that would make you break out in a cold sweat. Screams in the night. Goings-on in the bedrooms. Jiggery pokery in the pantry.
Herbert You oughtn't to speak like that you know. After all, he was your employer.
Gripe He wouldn't mind. A handsome feller he was, in his youth, with a roving eye and a ready wit. Ah well, he's gone now. God rest his wicked old soul.
Herbert Amen.
Gripe Left you this house, has he? The old devil. I bet he's having a good laugh now, wherever he is.

There is a piercing scream off UL

Herbert What was that!
Gripe I didn't 'ear nothing.
Herbert Someone screamed!
Gripe Oh, I thought you meant something unusual had happened.
Herbert (*moving quickly to the foot of the stairs*) It sounded like Alathea.
Gripe I don't take any notice of screams in this house. Nor will you when you've been here a bit longer.

Alathea screams again and hurriedly enters UL

Alathea Something touched my face in the dark! It was cold and hairy! It . . . it hissed in my ear!
Gripe I expect it was Mephistopheles.
Herbert What!
Gripe Or Beelzebub.
Herbert Who?
Gripe They're my two bats. I hope you didn't upset them, screaming like

Act I

that. Very sensitive things, bats ... easily frightened. You be careful and don't go disturbing them. I'd better see if they're all right. Coming in here, frightening other people's bats ...

Gripe exits UL, *grumbling to himself*

Alathea The place is a shambles. I'm beginning to think your Uncle Desmond must have been out of his mind.
Herbert Oh come, my dear. "De mortuis nil nisi bonum."

Belinda and Cyril come into view behind the leaded window

Alathea Thank heaven he lit the fire, anyway.

Belinda taps on the pane to attract their attention

There's Belinda. Go and open the door for her.
Herbert Yes, my dear.
Alathea And then carry the bags upstairs.

Herbert opens the door

Belinda (*off*) Hello, Daddy. What a spooky looking place.

Belinda enters, carrying a suitcase. She is sweet but shrewd

The outside's enough to give one the willies.

Cyril enters with another suitcase. He is an affable but fatuous young man

Cyril Hello, Mrs Budgett. There doesn't seem to be a garage so I've parked my little two-seater under a tree. How are you Mrs Budgett? Are you nicely settled in now?
Alathea That we are not. (*She draws the curtains across the window*)
Herbert Our train was over an hour late and we've only just arrived.
Alathea What's more we had to walk nearly a mile across the fields because there wasn't a taxi at the station. All we found was a ticket collector whose breath reeked of gin. There was no necessity for you to wish him a Merry Christmas in such an envious tone.
Herbert I'm sorry, my dear. It was merely a pleasantry on my part.

Cyril is wandering about examining the panelling etc

Cyril I say what a wonderful old place this is. Absolutely bung full of atmosphere. You can feel the past crawling up your spine. Laying its cold dead fingers on the back of your neck.
Alathea That reminds me, I must tell Gripe to air the beds.
Belinda Gripe? What's Gripe?
Alathea Gripe, I have just gathered, is the entire domestic staff.

Gripe enters UL

Gripe What! More of 'em!
Belinda Mother, you're joking. You surely don't mean there aren't any maids in the house?

Gripe Maids they may have been but the master made them into mistresses. (*He leers disgustingly*)

Gripe exits into the kitchen

Herbert That was Gripe.
Cyril Yes, it looked it.
Belinda Do you mean there's only that old man to do all the work about the place?
Herbert There seems to have been some misunderstanding.
Alathea Mr Gosforth said the butler would meet us on arrival, but that dreadful old man didn't seem to know anything about us.

Gripe enters with a long loaf of bread in his right pocket and a string of black puddings trailing from the left. He carries a tray containing plates and a tablecloth

Gripe I expect you'd like something to eat. I'm just seeing what we've got to be finished up.
Herbert Gripe, this is my daughter Belinda and this is Mr Carraway.
Gripe How do you do. (*He puts the tray on the table*) You're not staying are you? You don't want anything to eat do you?
Belinda Well, really . . .
Cyril I don't know about you darling, but I'm feeling pretty peckish. I could eat a horse.
Gripe (*putting the bread and black puddings on the table*) Oh no. We can't have that. I can't go killing off the livestock just for you. You'll have plain simple fare just like everybody else. (*He is about to exit into the kitchen*)
Alathea Just a moment. Why were you not expecting us? Weren't you given instructions by Mr Gosforth?
Gripe Gosforth? Who's he? Never heard of him.
Alathea Mr Gosforth is the late Mr Cheyney's solicitor. I understood that he had notified you of our intended arrival.
Herbert Do you mean to say that you had no communication from him?
Gripe Oh no. Nothing like that.
Cyril What's this doing here? (*He has found a long important-looking envelope in the tray of the umbrella stand*) Isn't your name Gripe? It's for you.
Gripe Oh yes; I've been looking for that. That came last week. (*He opens the envelope and takes out a letter*) I've been meaning to read it some time when I could find my glasses. 'Ere, you'll have to tell me what it says. (*He looks very closely at the envelope*) I can see the stamp. (*He turns his scrutiny to both sides of the letter*) But I can't make out which side the writing's on. (*He hands the letter to Cyril*)
Alathea This is impossible! He'll have to go. As soon as we can get somebody else.
Cyril This explains the whole thing. It tells you of Mr Cheyney's death, of his leaving the house to Mr Budgett and finally instructs you to have everything in readiness for their arrival. Mr Gosforth adds a postscript to the effect that he is coming down here tonight himself by the later train.

Act I

Gripe No ... No he can't do that.
Alathea Why not pray? There are plenty of bedrooms aren't there?
Gripe Yes, there's bedrooms in abundance, but they haven't been opened since the master left, fifteen years ago.
Alathea Then you'd better start getting them ready.
Gripe Unlock the chambers I will, and put warming pans in the beds. That's a good idea; it'll help to dry the sheets somewhat. More than that I cannot do. I'm very short handed. I've only got one pair. (*He turns to go*)
Alathea When you have finished preparing the meal, you will light the fires in all the rooms.
Gripe I couldn't do that. It wouldn't be a very nice thing to do. They wouldn't like it.
Herbert Who wouldn't like it?
Gripe The bats. They'd be very upset. (*To Alathea*) How would you like flames and smoke crackling through *your* winter quarters?

Gripe exits to the kitchen

Belinda Why is Mr Gosforth coming tonight?
Alathea It seems there were certain conditions attached to the legacy which were not to be made known until seven days after the reading of the will.
Cyril Doesn't anybody know what these conditions are?
Belinda With all that lovely money at stake it doesn't matter what they are. I'd run about without a stitch on in Selfridge's bargain basement rather than lose my share.
Alathea Really! Belinda!
Cyril You'd better see a psychiatrist.
Alathea Herbert, what are you doing?
Herbert (*at the telephone*) Nothing my dear. I was merely wondering if the telephone was in working order. One wouldn't wish to be cut off from the outside world.
Alathea Never mind about that. Make yourself useful. Go into the kitchen and scour out the saucepans.
Herbert Yes, my dear.
Alathea And clean the knives and forks; they're filthy.
Herbert Yes, my dear.
Alathea And get in between the prongs.
Herbert Yes, very well my dear, I will.
Alathea And then we shall need some more wood for the fire. You needn't think you're going to loaf about while you're down here.
Herbert Yes, my dear.
Alathea What did you say?
Herbert No, my dear.

Herbert exits to the kitchen

Belinda Poor Daddy.
Alathea (*removing the dust sheet from the settee*) Your father is a fundamental idler. (*She turns to Cyril*) All our married life I've had to tell him what to do. The only thing he ever wanted to do himself was to open a second-

hand bookshop. Of course, he would have been bankrupt inside a year and then what should we have done? But he couldn't see that. I had to stand over him and make him hold on to his job as a Civil Servant. You'd think he'd have been grateful to me, but oh no! I don't complain but it's very wearying to have a man leaning on you all the time.
Cyril Poor old Herbert.
Alathea What do you mean by that remark?
Cyril (*in confusion*) I only meant it must be very uncomfortable ... I mean, not being able to stand on his own two feet ... having someone else standing on them for him ... I think I'd better take these bags up. (*He picks up two suitcases*).
Belinda Come on Cyril, we'll go exploring.

Cyril starts to go up the stairs

(*At the foot of the stairs*) Let's take a look at Gripe's abundant bedrooms and chilly chambers. See you later, Mother. Don't be too hard on Daddy. He only wants a quiet life, you know.

Gripe enters DL *with a hunk of cheese in one hand and a log for the fire in the other*

You go first Cyril and scare away the bats.

The telephone rings

Who's this, I wonder? (*She lifts the receiver*)

Gripe is by the fire. He turns and listens

Hullo ... Who? Mr Budgett? ... Who's speaking? ... Oh! ... Well could you hold on? I'll get him to come to the phone. It's for Daddy.
Alathea Who is it?
Belinda She won't say. She says it's a surprise.
Alathea A woman! For Herbert!
Belinda (*at the kitchen door*) Daddy, you're wanted on the phone.

Herbert enters wearing a moth-eaten green baize apron

Herbert Are you sure it's for me? (*He takes the receiver*) Hullo ... Who? ... Flossie? ... ? Oh! ... Oh yes, of course, Flossie.
Alathea Flossie!
Herbert Yes, of course I remember. It's one of the things I try to forget ... No, no, I don't wish to be reminded of those hectic nights ... Yes, I do indeed. I also remember the time we fought each other with pillows.
Alathea Oh!
Herbert It wasn't very kind of you to lock me out all night in my pyjamas.
Alathea Pyjamas!
Herbert Yes, very well ... All right. Goodbye. (*He hangs up*)
Alathea Herbert!
Herbert Yes, my dear?
Alathea Who was that woman?
Herbert I don't understand you. It was only Ogleby.

Act I

Belinda You'd better own up Father. I'm afraid I let the cat out of the bag by telling Mother it was a woman on the phone.
Herbert Oh no, my dear. You're mistaken, I do assure you.
Alathea What were those references to pyjamas and pillow fights? Don't pretend you weren't expecting her to ring. Now I know why you were so concerned about the telephone.
Herbert No ... No this is a misconception! It was an old schoolfellow. Alec Ogleby. I was his fag at St Michael's.
Alathea I wasn't born yesterday.
Herbert Oh no, my dear. I know you weren't.
Alathea What!
Herbert You're under a misapprehension, my dear. We were chums at school. He was recalling horseplay in the dorm ... It isn't what you think at all.
Alathea How can you tell such lies! I heard you address her as Flossie.
Belinda It's no good, Daddy. I say, you're quite a dark horse aren't you?
Alathea It's a wise child that knows its own father!
Herbert No, my dear, it was Ogleby.
Alathea Then who was Flossie?
Herbert (*after a pause*) I was Flossie. It was a nickname bestowed upon me over thirty years ago. In my salad days.
Alathea I don't believe a word of it.
Herbert You can set your mind at rest. Ogleby will be here in a few minutes. He was telephoning from the *Rose and Crown* in the village. He wants to come and talk over old times.
Alathea Is this the truth?
Herbert I swear it.
Alathea I'm not a woman you can deceive easily.
Herbert (*to himself*) No, my dear. That's very true.
Alathea I'll speak to you later.

Alathea exits to the kitchen

Belinda Daddy, you've got yourself into a mess, haven't you?
Cyril (*eagerly*) Is she really coming here tonight?
Herbert It was only Ogleby! Why did you pretend it was a woman?
Belinda It's all right, Daddy. You don't have to keep up a front with me. I spoke to her on the phone. I know as well as you do that it was some fascinating witch of a woman.
Herbert But I swear ...
Belinda Don't worry, I'm on your side. I think it's a very good thing if you do kick over the traces now and then with some of your wild women friends.
Herbert You mustn't say such things! You'll get me into trouble! My life is an open book.
Cyril Some of the pages are a bit dog-eared.
Belinda We'll back you up, but it's a pity you hit on such an unlikely story. Come on Cyril, let's brave the dangers of the dark.
Cyril Good luck ... You'll need it when your girl friend turns up.

Belinda and Cyril exit UL

Gripe You're a lad, you are.
Herbert Certainly not. It's all a mistake.
Gripe If you want to get rid of the old battle-axe ... (*He nods towards the kitchen door*) ... I can always grind up some glass.
Herbert What do you mean?
Gripe That's the stuff to make 'em writhe and wriggle.
Herbert I don't understand you at all.
Gripe Snag is, you've got to get rid of 'em afterwards, and our boiler's not very big.
Herbert I trust I misinterpret you.
Gripe Acid's best but acid's expensive.

Gripe exits to the kitchen

Herbert What can I do! Poised between the hammer and the anvil! (*He sits right of the table*)

Bunny Tucker enters through the main door. She is a lovable little blonde with a generous nature. She wears an imitation fur coat which she is clasping together in a state of agitation. She is breathless as if she has been running

Bunny Thank goodness there's somebody here. I'm all out of breath.

Herbert rises in amazement

You look a nice little man. You'll take care of me, won't you?
Herbert What do you mean? What do you want?
Bunny I don't want to be a nuisance but I'm going to ask you to take me under your wing tonight.
Herbert Heavens! What are you suggesting?
Bunny You will, won't you?
Herbert Certainly not. I wouldn't do such a thing. I'm a married man. I ... I'm a father.
Bunny All the better. Then perhaps you'll lend a sympathetic ear to my problems. You see it's like this. I'm in trouble.
Herbert Good Heavens!
Bunny I'm really in a jam I can tell you.
Herbert Mercy me!
Bunny You see there's a man after me. With a tommyhawk. I'm going to ask you to do me the biggest favour a man can do for a girl.
Herbert I'm afraid it's not feasible. I won't comply.
Bunny Oh, you are a naughty man. You've got a wicked mind. I only meant I wanted you to put me up for the night without asking anything in return.
Herbert You want to stay here?
Bunny I've just got to. I'm in a desperate situation.
Herbert No! No, it would never do.
Bunny You won't refuse to help me, will you? You've got such a kind face. I don't know where else to turn. If he catches me again there's no knowing what he may do.

Act I   11

Herbert I find it difficult to follow you.
Bunny He said he'd cut my ears off and I believe he meant it. Look what he's done already. (*She slips one arm out of her fur coat and reveals that she has a large bruise on her right shoulder and also that she is dressed in a scanty two-piece cowgirl outfit, with bare midriff and a tasselled fringe*) Look!
Herbert No! No! You mustn't expose yourself to temptation!
Bunny You are funny. Shall I tell you something? I like you.
Herbert You mustn't say such things.
Bunny Why not? I mean it. I think you're cute.
Herbert This is not the place for dalliance. You must go. At once. Before we are surprised.

Herbert starts to bundle her towards the door. She does not want to go

Bunny What is there to be surprised about?

Alathea enters DL

Alathea Herbert! So this is the explanation!

Cyril and Belinda enter UL

Cyril Oh, I say! Caught in the act!
Herbert No! No! I'm utterly in the dark!
Alathea (*to Bunny*) What do you mean by coming here?
Bunny I've come to appeal for protection. This man's after me. He won't leave me alone. Look what he did to me yesterday. (*She exhibits more bruises*)
Cyril (*looking admiringly at Herbert*) What a man!
Belinda He did that?
Alathea And he said he took the dog for a walk! The beast!
Bunny He said he'd kill me if I told anyone about it but I don't care. I've got bruises everywhere ...

Bunny is about to reveal them but Herbert forestalls her, closing her coat in panic

Herbert It's a plot! It never happened!
Alathea Do you deny that what this woman says is true?
Bunny You won't let him get hold of me again will you?
Herbert I tell you my conscience is clear!
Bunny (*puzzled*) I daresay it is. I didn't say it wasn't. But that doesn't help me very much, does it? (*To Alathea*) You won't let him get me alone again will you? He's terrible when he's roused. Just like a wild beast. He does whatever comes into his head. There's no stopping him. I just couldn't stand it ... not twice nightly.
Herbert I'm innocent. I swear it.
Alathea Is this unfortunate woman the one you spoke to on the telephone? Or is it yet another? You Jekyll and Hyde! How many more skeletons are there in your cupboard?
Herbert I have never set eyes on this lady before.

Alathea You scoundrel!
Bunny Hey, wait a minute. What's going on here?
Alathea Men like you should be put away. You're not fit for decent society.
Bunny Hold everything. I'm not talking about this little man.
Alathea What! but you've just told us how he beat you, how he bruised you...
Bunny Jumping Jelly Babies, no! You've got it all wrong. It was Thundercloud.

There is a blank silence

The knife thrower... the Red Indian.
Alathea (*faintly*) Red... Indian...?
Bunny Well he's Greek really.
Herbert There my dear, you see? I wish you weren't so ready to think ill of me.
Belinda Cyril, I think you'd better try to sort this out.
Cyril I'll have a shot at it. Who's this knife thrower chap? Where is he?
Bunny Search me. I don't know. That's the worrying thing about it. He chased me through the woods but I gave him the slip.
Alathea Where have you come from?
Bunny Hackenschmidt's Big Top.
Cyril I beg yours? Who's what?
Bunny Hackenschmidt's Big Top. We're performing over Christmas. "Every night at five and eight, matinees at two-thirty. Come early and be sure of a seat".
Cyril Ah, the penny drops! The circus.
Belinda That's right. We saw that big coloured poster by the Town Hall.
Cyril And he's chasing you? This knife-throwing Thundercloud?
Bunny He certainly is.
Belinda Why?
Bunny Well, he's been drinking and I wasn't going to stand there in front of all those people and let him do what he said he was going to do. So I ran away right in the middle of the act.
Herbert What did he say he was going to do?
Bunny He said he'd throw his last knife at the bullseye.
Cyril Could you explain? I think I see what you mean but perhaps I'm wrong.
Bunny It's enough to make anyone run away. (*To Alathea*) How would you feel? You see it's like this. I stand against this big dartboard thing and he throws knives all around me. Like he's playing darts, see? First he throws one at double six and then double seven and so on until he's scored two hundred and fifty. Tonight he said he'd only go up to two hundred and then... bullseye!
Herbert Oh, you poor little thing!
Cyril What a cad's trick! Don't you worry, we'll see he doesn't bother you again, little girl. (*He is patting her hand*) My name's Cyril.
Bunny I'm Bunny Tucker. Pleased to meet you.

Act I

Cyril It's a good thing you came here where you'll be more or less safe. A very good thing. (*He goes on patting*) A very good thing indeed.

Belinda Don't let me interrupt the growth of a beautiful friendship. But hadn't we better decide what's to be done? Supposing the knife-thrower comes here looking for his target?

Cyril (*still patting*) Yes, we'll have to hide the dartboard. Charming little dartboard.

Herbert (*absent-mindedly stroking Bunny's hair*) Gripe can always open another bedroom.

Alathea She can't very well spend the night here.

Herbert I don't see why not, my dear. She certainly can't go back to the circus.

Alathea You're not seriously suggesting this woman should stay here all night?

Herbert There are bedrooms in abundance.

Alathea That's hardly the point. And stop doing that!

Herbert abruptly stops stroking Bunny's hair

Bunny Please, look, I don't want to cause any inconvenience. Perhaps if you could just let me stay here for a little while in case he's hanging around outside waiting for me to come out.

Belinda Did he see you come in?

Bunny I don't know. If he did he may come knocking at your door at any minute.

Herbert Oh indeed! Have no fear. If this scoundrel comes here he'll have me to reckon with!

There is a thunderous knocking at the centre door. A moment of silence

Cyril It's the day of reckoning.

Thundercloud hurls Greek abuse at them through the door

Bunny It's him! He's terrible when he's full of drink!

Alathea (*backing away from the door apprehensively*) Oh! How disgusting!

Bunny You won't let him take me away will you?

Alathea (*opening the kitchen door*) I wash my hands of the whole business.

Thundercloud roars and beats on the door once more

I can't stand this. Get rid of that dreadful drunken person at once!

Alathea exits to the kitchen

Belinda Quick! We must tuck Miss Tucker away somewhere. (*She comes quickly to the stairs*) You'd better come with me.

Bunny (*to Cyril and Herbert*) I don't know how to thank you. Really I don't. You've both been so kind.

Cyril kisses Bunny's hand gallantly. Bunny pats Herbert's cheek. Herbert beams

There is a prolonged pounding on the door

   Belinda and Bunny hurriedly exit up the stairs

Cyril (*swallowing*) Will you open it or shall I?
Herbert (*nervously*) It's immaterial. You can if you want to.
More knocking and bellowing from Thundercloud
Cyril I tell you what. I'll open it and tell him you've got a bone to pick with him.
Herbert I think it would be better if you told him to come back tomorrow.
Cyril unbolts the door and opens it
Cyril Not today, thank you.

Cyril closes the door and leans against it mopping his brow. But he has omitted to shoot the bolt and the door is violently pushed open again sending Cyril flying

   Thundercloud enters. He is a very big man dressed as a Red Indian chief, wearing a huge feather head-dress and brandishing a tomahawk

Thundercloud (*brushing Cyril aside and towering above Herbert*) Where is she? What have you done with her?
Herbert She's where you won't find her.
Cyril Yes, she is. So just paddle your wares elsewhere.
Herbert And in your own canoe too.
Thundercloud Don't play the fool with me! (*He crosses to Cyril and shakes him, lifting him off the floor with one hand*) Give her back to me or I will slit your nostrils for you!
Cyril (*to Herbert, his toes scrabbling*) I think this is your department. (*To Thundercloud*) This is our Mr Budgett.
Thundercloud Speak! Or I tear out your tongue!
Herbert (*tapping him on the shoulder*) Just one moment. Kindly stop throwing your weight around will you?

   Belinda and Bunny peer round the top of the stairs and cautiously watch the rest of the scene

Thundercloud What do you say to me!
Cyril You come in here ... without taking your hat off ... breathing fire-water all over the furniture ...
Thundercloud You will be sorry you speak!
Herbert You can't expect people to like you if you carry on like this you know.
Cyril You go about throwing knives at people's bullseyes ... you're old enough to know better.
Herbert Go away and don't you dare bring your twice-nightly habits here again!
Thundercloud You talk to me like this? I am Thundercloud of the hundred knives. I spit on you! (*He does*)

Act I

Herbert You'll go too far if you go any further.
Cyril Listen, Running Water, we don't like your face and we don't fancy your feathers.
Thundercloud I know what you are after. You are wanting to keep her for yourself, eh?
Herbert Enough of that! If you're not out of here in half a minute I'll ring up the police and have you arrested for committing a nuisance.
Thundercloud Oh yes! That we shall see. (*He moves menacingly towards them*)
Cyril (*hurriedly lifting the telephone receiver*) Are you going?
Thundercloud Very well. I go.
Cyril Good.
Thundercloud But I come back!
Cyril Bad.
Thundercloud And I bring with me my big brothers. My brother, Alexis, he is the strong man, he bend the iron bars with his teeth. My brother, Leopoldo, he fight with tigers and crocodiles. Together we fix you. And I bring with me Zambazi the giant with two heads. I will bring ...
Cyril You can bring Hackenschmidt and his big top as well for all we care. So there. (*He snaps his fingers unsuccessfully*)
Herbert We don't care how many heads your friends have.
Cyril We just don't give a fig for them.
Thundercloud Soon you will be sorry we meet. If she is not back by midnight your flesh will hang in strips.
Cyril And a witch's curse on you too.

Thundercloud exits slamming the door

Cyril hurriedly bolts it behind him

Belinda (*coming down the stairs*) Congratulations Daddy! Cyril, you were terrific!
Cyril Thank you darling. I was rather, wasn't I?
Belinda You were wonderful, Daddy.
Bunny I'm ever so grateful. No one's ever stood up to him like that before.
Cyril Aw shucks, 'twern't nothin'.
Bunny (*to Herbert*) You were ever so brave. (*To Cyril*) He might have split your head open with that wicked-looking tommyhawk.
Cyril It was nothing at all ... I feel sick! (*He sits abruptly in the chair above the table*)
Belinda Do you think he meant what he said? About coming back with his brothers. They sounded pretty grim.
Bunny I'm afraid so. Of course they're only his half-brothers really, but they're as thick as thieves and their blood is thicker than water.
Cyril We'll deal with the brothers grim when they arrive. In the meantime ...

Gripe enters DL *followed by Alathea. Gripe carries knives and forks which he puts on the table*

Herbert Ah, there you are, Gripe. Will you prepare another room. We have an unexpected guest in Miss Tucker. She will be staying the night.
Gripe This is quite like old times. If only the master were here.
Herbert That will do, Gripe. I want none of this familiarity. Miss Tucker is a guest. Kindly remember that and treat her accordingly.
Gripe Very well, sir.

Gripe exits to the kitchen

Alathea What's happened to you, Herbert Budgett? It's not like you to start giving orders. (*She turns to Bunny*) Why did you have to select this house as a refuge? We shall all have our throats cut before the night is out.
Bunny Oh dear, I'm sorry if . . .
Herbert You're very welcome I assure you. This is, after all, the season of goodwill.
Bunny I think that's ever so sweet of you, Mr Budgett. That's ever such a nice thing to say. You're a real gentleman, that's what you are.
Alathea I shall have something to say to you, Herbert, when we're alone. Don't try my patience too far!
Herbert I . . . (*He seems about to remonstrate and then subsides*) No, my dear.
Belinda I'll show you the way. Would you like me to lend you a dress for the rest of the evening? And I think I've a spare pyjama suit for you to sleep in.
Bunny Thanks loads. You're a good sort.
Cyril (*rising eagerly*) I have a tube of toothpaste you can share.
Bunny I'm sorry to give you all this trouble. I think I'm ever so lucky to have fallen on my feet. Well, if you'll excuse me. Bye-bye boys. See you later. (*She catches Alathea's eye and gives a friendly wave of the hand*) Toodle-oo, Mrs Budgett.

Bunny exits followed by Belinda, and leaving the "boys" beaming after her

Alathea I'm going to unpack my things. You go back into the kitchen.

There is a knocking at the door

Cyril (*in a panic*) There's a man with two heads at the door!
Alathea It may be Mr Gosforth.
Herbert Or Alec Ogleby.
Alathea That I very much doubt. I'll believe in this old schoolfellow of yours when I see him but not before.

Cyril opens the door

Gosforth (*in the doorway*) Ah, good evening. I'm Gosforth of Gosforth and Strokelady. Are the Budgetts within?
Cyril Yes, they're expecting you. Come on in.

Gosforth enters. He is a legal gentleman, bowler-hatted and pin-stripe trousered. He has a habit of clearing his throat nervously

Alathea Mr Gosforth. How good of you to come down.

Gosforth My dear lady. Not at all. I had intended to delay my visit until after the festive season but I knew you'd be on tenterhooks. (*He crosses to the fire and warms his posterior*) We shall have more snow before long I fear. Good evening, Mr Budgett. The compliments of the season to you.
Herbert Thank you. The same to you.
Gosforth I'm glad to see you're settling in without any trouble. Is everything going smoothly? Good. Good. You'll find it very quiet and peaceful down here I expect. It's a sleepy little place. It won't seem very exciting after London.
Cyril Oh, I don't know.
Gosforth I daresay the local people will leave you very much alone for the first few months. You won't have any strangers knocking at your door. Oh, there's just one thing. I hope it won't inconvenience you but there isn't another train back to London until the day after tomorrow. Perhaps you could be kind enough to shake me down over Christmas.

Gripe enters from the kitchen with soup plates for the table

Herbert Why yes, of course ... Gripe ...
Alathea Gripe, Mr Gosforth is staying the night.
Gripe I'll unlock another chamber.
Cyril How much longer is this meal of yours going to be?
Gripe I'd have had it on the table by now only I have to keep chasing the mice away. It's the smell of food you know. It brings 'em out.
Alathea Mice! In the kitchen!
Gripe Yes. They're after my special soup.
Alathea This is terrible. Can't you get rid of them?
Gripe I've tried. We had a cat once but they ate it.
Alathea You must get some traps.
Gripe I got some traps. I put them down only a fortnight ago. I'll see if I've caught anything yet. (*He exits but puts his head back tround the door again*) Supper won't be long.

Gripe finally goes

Cyril I don't like the sound of that.
Alathea I'm so sorry about this, Mr Gosforth. As soon as Christmas is over I shall get rid of that terrible old creature and engage a housekeeper.
Gosforth Perhaps you should hear the further conditions of Mr Cheyney's will first. One of the clauses concerns Gripe.
Herbert Concerns Gripe? In what way?
Gosforth I think I'd better wait until after supper before I read you the codicil, that is to say the additional clauses which modify the terms of the will.
Alathea But I don't understand. Surely ...

There is a knocking at the door

Herbert This will be Ogleby.
Alathea It had better be Ogleby.

Cyril It's your turn.

Herbert opens the door

Lydia (*in the doorway*) Hullo. I hope I didn't ring up at an awkward moment.
Alathea I thought so! Now what have you to say? So this is your Flossie!
Lydia Who, me? Oh no. My name's Lydia.
Cyril What! Another one! How many more have you got?
Lydia Who's Flossie anyway?

Lydia enters and smiles at Cyril. She is tall, dark, attractive and sophisticated

Alathea Is *this* the woman you spoke to? Answer me!
Herbert Dearest, I don't understand. I spoke only to Ogleby.
Alathea Don't try to deceive me!
Lydia (*to Cyril*) What's all the fuss about?
Alathea (*to Lydia*) Will you deny that you spoke to my husband on the telephone?
Lydia Certainly I will. I rang up and asked for Mr Budgett, somebody went to fetch him and I handed the 'phone over to Alec.
Alathea Alec . . . ?
Lydia Alec Ogleby. Surely you've heard of him? He's a well-known film producer. I'm his secretary.

Alec is heard off, singing "The Twelve Days Of Christmas"

If you don't believe me you'd better ask him. Here he comes.

Alec Ogleby breezes in, bearing a Christmas tree, several gaily-wrapped parcels and two carrier bags containing bottles of whisky, Christmas puddings, turkeys, etc. In his mouth is a large cigar and in his heart goodwill to all mankind. He breathes the companionable spirit of the Rose and Crown *and is very merry. He is hearty and expansive and possessed of a roving eye*

Alec Hello everybody! Hello! Hello! Hello! Flossie old boy! Well, well, well! (*He deposits his parcels on the table with Cyril's help, and pumps Herbert's hand vigorously*) After all these years, eh? It's good to see you again. I read in the paper about you taking over this old place and I thought, "Good old Flossie. I'll ring him up and surprise him" (*He breaks into song again*) "Christmas comes but once a year". (*He is unpacking bottle after bottle from the carrier bags and from the capacious pockets of his overcoat*) "And when it comes there's lots of beer. Hi-ti-tiddley-ti." How do everybody. (*He waves his hand cheerily*) I'm Alec Ogleby. You're all my friends. I've brought you all presents. Big-hearted Alec. That's what they call me in Wardour Stret. The most open-handed man in pictures. We were at school together you know. Flossie used to fag for me. Happy days at the old college. Good old Flossie. Hasn't changed a bit. Still the same old Flossie. Have a cigar. (*He thrusts a huge cigar into Herbert's mouth and slaps him heartily on the back. He suddenly sees Alathea*) Forgive me.

Act I

Forgive me, I didn't recognize you for the moment. It *is* Mrs Budgett, isn't it? Mrs Budgett. There you see, what a memory.

Alathea I don't think we've ...

Alec Ah, you don't remember me but I remember you. I remember you used to come down on speech days wearing a gay hat with flowers on it. (*He turns to Herbert*) Your mother doesn't look a day older. Wonderful. (*He shakes her hand warmly*) I don't know how you do it.

Alathea Well, really ... !

Alec Here's something to keep the cold out. Champagne. Champagne for everybody. Lavish. Lavish. That's what we are in the film business. Hang the expense. (*He presses a goose into Alathea's arms*) There's a fine fat goose. You can stuff that for tomorrow. You don't mind putting us up for the night, do you? Christmas at Creeping Cheyney! (*He bursts into song again*) "Christmas comes but once a year. Hi-ti-tiddley-ti!"

There is an ear-splitting interruption as Gripe enters from the kitchen, hugging a large soup tureen in his left arm and wielding a football rattle. Belinda enters UL

Gripe Supper's ready. (*He places the tureen on the table*) There's a nice meat stew in there. Don't let it get cold. Good thing I put them traps down. (*He produces two dead mice from his pockets*) I'll just nip upstairs and feed me bats.

The Women scream

Bunny enters UL

Holding the corpses by their tails Gripe makes his way upstairs. Bunny flees in terror before him.

The Women are still screaming as

The CURTAIN *falls*

ACT II

Scene 1

One hour later

Gosforth stands behind the table, pincenez on nose and a sealed document in his hand. Herbert is seated right of the table and Alathea to the left of it. Belinda is in the left end of the couch with Cyril on her right. Alec is perched on the left arm of the settee, Lydia on the right arm. Bunny sits on the US end of the firestool. All except Herbert and Alathea have glasses of Alec's whisky in their hands, the men are smoking Alec's cigars. Gripe, a seedy napkin over his arm, hovers in the background like a Dickensian wine waiter

Supper has been cleared away but on the table are dishes of fruit, a bowl of nuts and a pair of nutcrackers

As the CURTAIN *rises there is a general chorus of "Hear! Hear!" "Good old Ogleby!" "Three cheers for Ogleby!"*

Gosforth Our thanks are indeed due to Mr Ogleby. But for his timely arrival, bearing seasonal gifts, the groaning board might have presented a ... shall I say, a less festive appearance. I ask you to raise your glasses to that distinguished impresario of the cinematic industry, Mr Alec Ogleby.
All Hear! Hear! Good old Ogleby! *(etc)*
Gosforth Furthermore, I should like to take this opportunity of wishing you all the very best of health on this doubly festive occasion. May fortune smile upon you and may you long live to enjoy the fruits of your Uncle's beneficence.
All Hear Hear! Hear Hear!
Gosforth As you already know, the yearly allowance is a generous one. Even allowing for deductions from the sum total of the estate ... death duties and so forth ... it should still attain to between fifty and sixty thousand pounds per person per annum.

There is a chorus of approval and congratulation

Cyril Congratulations Mr Budgett. And you, Mrs Budgett ... And you, darling.
Bunny Oh my goodness, isn't it lovely for you? I couldn't be more pleased unless it was me.
Alec You lucky lot of Budgetts! What are you going to do with your share, Flossie?
Herbert Well ... I had thought of ...
Alathea If you don't mind Mr Ogleby, we'd like to hear the details.

Act II, Scene 1

Alec Eh? ... Oh sorry.
Alathea Proceed Mr Gosforth.
Gosforth We now come to the conditions laid down by Mr Cheyney in his instructions to me. (*He breaks the seal of the envelope*)

There is a general stir of interest

> (*Clearing his throat in an alarming manner*) "I Desmond Cheyney of Womba Womba in the Queensland province of Australia, being of sound mind and in full possession of all my faculties, do make and declare this to be codicil to my last will and testament. Whereas I have in and by my said will given and bequeathed unto my nephew Herbert Oswald Budgett and his wife Alathea Wilhelmina Budgett and their daughter Belinda Brenda Budgett a legacy, in the form of an annual payment to each in equal sums for the remainder of their natural lives, I do hereby set forth certain conditions governing the continuance of the said legacies, viz and to whit: One: that the aforementioned legatees do reside in the house known as Creeching Cheyney in the county of Hampshire, nightly, for the term of one entire year, commencing on the night of December twenty-fourth next."

Alathea Why does he insist on that particular date? Why December the twenty-fourth?
Gosforth Well, Mrs Budgett, I believe this clause is intended as a ... well, in a sense, a test of character. You see the house is locally reputed to be untenable, in fact uninhabitable at certain times of the year.
Alathea What do you mean?
Gosforth It is said to be haunted by ghosts.
Alec (*in surprise*) Ghosts!
Bunny (*in a squeak*) Ghosts!
Alathea (*scornfully*) Ghosts!
Cyril (*a little after the others*) G ... ghosts?
Herbert You mean apparitions?
Bunny (*helpfully*) Bogies?

Gripe moves down to refill Cyril's glass

Gosforth It seems there are certain seasons of the year when the various ... ah ... spectres are said to appear, one such occasion being the night of Christmas Eve.
Belinda Tonight!
Alathea Ridiculous.
Cyril (*nervously*) You mean there's supposed to be a family ghost at Creeching Cheyney? Why, that's just a lot of nonsense.

Cyril laughs apprehensively but his laughter is cut short as he suddenly finds Gripe's face close to his own

Gripe It's like the crackling of thorns under a pot.
Cyril What is?
Gripe (*moving away*) The laughter of fools.
Cyril There's no need to be personal.
Alec You're not suggesting there's any truth in it?

Gripe It's true all right. And there's more than one.
Lydia You mean there are ghosts in the plural?
Gripe Aye, and in the upstairs bedrooms too. There's the spirit of Montague Cheyney, him that died on the scaffold in fifteen seventy three. He always comes here to spend Christmas with his old friends.
Cyril (*in alarm*) How old are his friends?
Gripe Then there's Benjamin Cheyney. He usually drops in for a few nights round about the middle of Feb.
Cyril What happened to him?
Gripe (*with a descriptive gesture*) 'Anged. At Tyburn. Jan the fourth, seventeen twenty. It was a cold wintry morning. It rained all the time.
Belinda How do you know?
Alec I expect he was there.
Gripe Then there's Humphrey Cheyney who cut his throat in the Blue Room.
Alec Now wait a moment. Look here Creech ... Crutch ... (*He turns to Herbert*) What's his name again?
Herbert Gripe.
Alec Oh yes. Well now, look here Gripe, nobody believes in ghosts nowadays. You don't really expect us to swallow these yarns do you? They're just old wives' tales.
Alathea Of course they are. Superstitious gossip. Now, Mr Gosforth ...
Gripe Gossip is it! Gossip it isn't! I could tell you things ... but no. My lips are sealed. (*He fixes Alec with a baleful look*). You'll find out soon enough.
Alec What do you mean?
Gripe I've put you in the Blue Room.
Alec (*in alarm*) What's that got to do with it?
Gripe Ah! (*He turns away*)
Alec Hey, wait a minute, I don't ...
Alathea Will you kindly allow Mr Gosforth to continue! Do go on Mr Gosforth. We're all ears.
Gosforth Clause Number Two reads as follows. "That during his sojourn in the house my nephew Herbert Oswald Budgett shall drink one pint tankard of the rightly famed Creeching Claret nightly before retiring ... the said pint tankard to be drawn by the butler Gripe from the Creeching vaults."
Alec This gets better all the time, doesn't it?
Alathea I positively forbid it. I will not have Herbert drinking intoxicating liquor. I've never allowed it and I won't allow it now.
Alec Shame.
Gosforth I'm afraid Mrs Budgett that the late Mr Cheyney's wishes must be obeyed. His instructions are quite definite. Failure to comply with any of the terms of the codicil would nullify the entire bequest, as you will see. The money would then be bestowed elsewhere. However I mustn't anticipate.
Alathea You mean that Herbert is to be allowed to ...
Gosforth I'll proceed to Clause Three. "During their twelve months residence at Creeching Cheyney, the legatees shall be gentle with Gripe."

Act II, Scene 1   23

Gripe smirks

    "They shall have regard for his infirmities and they shall treat him with the courtesy and respect to which his age and faithful service entitle him."
Alathea Well . . . really! Gentle with Gripe indeed!
Gosforth Clause Number Four. "My nephew's daughter Belinda Budgett shall enter upon a state of lawful wedlock before the expiry of the twelve months residence."
Belinda What!
Bunny How romantic! I can see you all in white.
Belinda Don't! You make me sound like one of the family ghosts.
Cyril No more wild oats for you, darling. Awful wedlock.
Belinda But who am I going to find to marry if I have to spend every night here?
Cyril Well, there is me.
Belinda Don't be idiotic Cyril. You're just one of the wild oats I mustn't have any more of. (*To Gosforth*) What happens if I remain a bachelor girl? Don't I get any money?
Gosforth I'm afraid not, Miss Budgett. Not a penny.
Gripe (*to Herbert*) Would you like a drop of whisky sir? To celebrate?
Alathea Certainly not. Put that glass down, Herbert. And don't fiddle with your napkin. I've told you before.
Gosforth And now we come to Clause Number Five . . . which I fear may not be altogether to your liking Mrs Budgett. (*He clears his throat again and adjusts his spectacles*) "During the aforesaid twelvemonth my nephew Herbert Budgett shall cease to be browbeaten and defeated in argument by his wife Alathea Budgett and shall constantly remind her both by word and action that whereas he is that paragon of all the species, a male animal, she is but a female, fitted by nature to submit to her lawful husband, meek and obedient to his wishes; it being her task and duty to minister to his needs and . . ." ahem ". . . bring solace to his bed."

There is a stunned silence, broken by a guffaw from Alec and then general consternation

Alathea This is ridiculous!
Cyril Oh my godfathers!

Gripe is cackling

Alathea It's monstrous! Disgraceful! I won't be insulted like this! The old fool must have been in his dotage. Stop playing with the nuts, Herbert! That idiotic clause must be set aside.
Gosforth I'm afraid that cannot be, Mrs Budgett. Mr Cheyney's wishes, though admittedly eccentric, cannot, I repeat, be disregarded. Unless, that is, you wish your share of the money to be disposed of elsewhere.
Alathea But surely . . .
Gosforth Let me read you Mr Cheyney's own words on the matter. "If, by default, any of these conditions be not adhered to, then I do hereby

ordain that all subsequent payments shall be discontinued as regards the legatee or legatees referred to by name in this clause or clauses concerned ..."

Herbert May I ask ...

Alathea (*abruptly*) Be quiet!

Gosforth "And be transferred instead to Emily Makepeace Budgett, spinster of Kirkcaldy in the county of Fifeshire."

Alathea That woman!

Belinda Old Emily? The black sheep of the Budgetts?

Alathea I've never heard anything so intolerable. I suppose this is that wicked old devil's idea of a practical joke. In any case who's to judge whether or not the conditions of that last clause are kept? It's entirely a family matter.

Gosforth That, too, has been taken into consideration. "I leave the responsibility of ensuring the observance of these conditions to the faithful old friend and servitor already referred to, who is to report to my legal representative any failure to adhere to or attempt at avoidance of the aforementioned conditions and whose testimony in all such matters shall be final and binding." (*He folds the document deliberately*)

There is an astonished silence. All look at Gripe

Gripe He means me ... Mr Gripe.

Alathea Do I understand that we are to be spied upon by this decrepit old ...

Belinda Careful Mother! Remember clause three ... be gentle with Gripe. Courtesy, respect and all that.

Alathea Oh! (*She is almost beyond words*) OH! ... Herbert!

Herbert Yes, my dear?

Alathea Don't sit there with that dreamy look on your face! I suppose you imagine you're going to have your own way now in everything, do you?

Herbert Why no, my dear. I just ...

Alathea Because if you do I shall have to disillusion you. Some are fitted by nature to lead and others to follow. Let there be no misunderstanding in your mind on that point!

Gosforth (*consulting his watch*) It's been an eventful day. It's later than I thought. You'll forgive me if I make my way to bed. I'll leave you to discuss the matter at your leisure.

Belinda I think we'd all better sleep on it. I'm too tired to start looking for a husband tonight.

Gosforth Good night to you all.

Gosforth exits upstairs to a chorus of "Goodnight" and a scraping back of chairs

Alathea I'm going up now Herbert. I expect you to follow in ten minutes. You needn't think you're going to sit up all night staring into the fire, planning a life of self indulgence. In ten minutes, you understand? I want to have a little talk with you.

Alathea exits upstairs

Act II, Scene 1   25

Gripe You won't forget your nightcap, sir? One pint of the rightly famed.
Herbert Oh yes, of course.
Lydia I'm for the old fourposter. Ghost or no ghost I shall sleep like a log. It's been an entertaining evening but now it's time to hang up my stocking. I only hope there's nothing gruesome in it in the morning.
Bunny Aren't you afraid of the ghosts?
Lydia (*yawning*) I'm so sleepy the ghost of Montague Cheyney can get into bed beside me for all I care. (*She crosses to the stairs*) Provided he keeps his knees to himself. Goodnight everybody.

Lydia exits upstairs

Bunny I don't believe in spooks. But I'll keep the light on all night just in case. I can't make up my mind whether to keep my door shut to stop them getting in, or leave it open to let them go out. Goodnight all.

Bunny exits upstairs

Cyril (*opening the curtains a little and peering out into the night*) It's still snowing. Coming down thick and fast.
Belinda I say, Gripe, any chance of a bath?
Gripe Yes, there's been a grumbling noise in the pipes for the last half hour.
Cyril That's a jolly good idea. I could do with a bath.
Alec (*who has been busy with the whisky*) So could I.
Gripe There ought to be enough to fill a bath all right.
Cyril Oh, good.
Gripe If you don't mind sharing it among the lot of you.
Alec Eh?
Gripe Of course, it'll be a bit mucky by the time the last one gets in.
Cyril You don't mean we'll have to make one bathful of water do for all of us!
Alec Now look here, Croup ... Grope ...
Gripe There'll only be enough to fill it up once.
Belinda Cyril, you're too clean already and Mr Ogleby of the roving eye looks far too flushed to risk getting wet all over. I'll give you a shout when I'm out.

Belinda exits upstairs

Cyril Remarkable girl, your daughter, sir. A chip off the old block. Quite ruthless.
Herbert I beg your pardon?
Cyril I was thinking of your wife, sir, I didn't mean to imply that she was a chip off *your* old block. I've been turning something over.

Alec brings a suitcase from near the door and puts it on the table

Herbert You've been doing what?
Cyril Over in my mind I mean. I want to ask your formal permission. Will that be all right, sir?
Herbert (*still occupied with his own thoughts*) I'm sorry, what were you talking about?

Cyril Your daughter, sir.
Herbert Mmm? What about her?
Cyril I want to know if you'd mind having me for a father-in-law. No! I mean would you mind very much if I married your daughter?
Herbert (*elsewhere*) Yes, do by all means.
Cyril Oh good. That's all right then. I'll go and tell her now while the iron is hot. Excuse me.

Cyril exits upstairs

Alec (*producing a hot water bottle from his suitcase*) I say ... Sunny Jim. Perhaps you could pop a kettle on for this. I don't wish to deprive the young woman of steam.
Gripe I keep a cauldron going on me 'ob.
Alec On your 'ob? Well, in that case just you fill that up for me, will you? (*He hands Gripe the bottle*) There's a good Gripe. Aha! Got it straight that time didn't I?

Gripe exits DL

Alec That fellow Creep gives me the gripes.
Herbert (*rising to the surface and making for bed*) If you'll excuse me ...
Alec (*pushing him down again with a hand on his shoulder*) Just one moment old boy. I want to have a word in your ear while we're alone together. First of all my sincere congratulations on your good fortune. The question is "What are you going to do with all this cash?" Now, I'd like to do you a good turn so I'll tell you what I'll do.
Alathea (*off; distantly*) Herbert! How much longer are you going to be?
Alec Blast!
Herbert I shall have to go up I'm afraid. (*He rises*) She's in rather a funny mood tonight.
Alec Yes, I noticed that. All right, you go up and pacify her and then come down again and have a talk with me. Tell her you haven't had your Creeching Claret yet. Well, you haven't, have you? I'm going upstairs anyway ... (*he picks up the case*) ... but I'll see you down here again in about five minutes.
Herbert Well I ...
Alec Good.

Alec takes Herbert by the arm and moves towards the stairs

What I have to tell you is very much to your advantage. You were a good friend to me in days gone by.
Herbert Was I?
Alec Were you? You certainly were! I've always wanted to repay the debt I owe you and now I can pay you back in your own coin. That's just a figure of speech, of course.

Alec and Herbert exit upstairs

Thundercloud's face, suffused with rage and drink, appears at the window,

Act II, Scene 1   27

> glares through the gap in the curtains and quickly ducks down out of sight as:
>
> Belinda enters, followed by Cyril. Belinda is wearing a dressing gown over pyjamas

Belinda I expect it will all seem very simple in the morning but at the moment I can't quite get the hang of your conversation. You're leading up to something I suppose but there are other matters on my mind. I've got to think of a way of unearthing a suitable mate. (*She starts unpacking towels, sponge bag, etc, from her suitcase*)

Cyril But darling, that's what I'm trying to tell you. I'll make an honest woman of you with the best will in the world.

Belinda (*regarding him shrewdly*) Yes, it is quite a good one, isn't it?

Cyril Darling, I didn't mean I wanted your windfalls. I mean, after all, what is money really? It's just an awful nuisance, that's all it is ... a deep-rooted evil at the bottom of our ... (*he searches for the right word*) ... well ...

Belinda (*mystified*) Our well?

Cyril Well, our social system. (*He thumps the table with his fist*) That's what's the trouble with the whole of the British (*thump*) Fiscal (*thump*) policy. (*thump*)

Belinda What is?

Cyril Money. Darling, will you marry me? Don't give me your answer tonight. Any old time will do. Right now if you like. Will or no will, do say you will because it doesn't make any difference to me, really it doesn't. I'll never hold your filthy lucre against you ... nasty horrid stuff. Ugh! Tainted. I'll never reproach you with it. It's just that I couldn't bear to be without it ... No! I mean without you! Darling. (*Seizing her hand and kissing it*) Shall we tell them now or break it to them gently?

Belinda What are you blathering about? You haven't mistaken me for Father Christmas by any chance have you?

Cyril Pardon?

Belinda Hang up your socks at the end of your bed by all means but you won't find me putting sixty thousand a year in them.

Cyril Oh, but sweetheart, come now! We mustn't come to our bridges before we cross them ...

Belinda No Cyril. I don't want to hurt your feelings but I don't fancy myself as Mrs Carraway somehow.

Cyril You don't! Darling, you're not turning me down flat are you?

Belinda As a pancake. Sorry Cyril. (*She blows him a kiss*)

Belinda exits

Cyril Oh, but darling, try to put myself in your shoes ...

Cyril follows Belinda out

Thundercloud enters bearing a huge bow and a quiver of arrows and exits upstairs

Alec enters UL *and goes to his overcoat which is hanging on the coat rack, for his cigar case. He hums happily to himself*

Alec (*singing*) "We're in the money, the skies are sunny, pom-pom-pom-tiddley-om-pom-pom-pom."

Trimming a cigar he is oblivious of the fact that a small panel has opened in the flat beside him. An arm in a long black glove, holding a dagger, is waiting for him to step back into range

Alec moves away from the coat rack to the table

The arm is withdrawn and the panel closes

Lydia enters UL *in pyjamas and dressing-gown*

Lydia How's it going?
Alec I've broken the ice. He's coming down for his claret cup in a few minutes. I'll put it to him then.
Lydia Listen Alec, I've got something to say and I'm perfectly serious about it. Business is business I know, none better. But I hope you really are going to make this film Alec. I hope so for Herbert's sake.
Alec Don't worry. I'm not a crook. I've made films before, haven't I? Good ones too ... some of them were, anyway ... and I will again. You know how it's been. Up at the top one minute and down the drain the next. If I can only get enough capital to start all over again I'll be turning them out bigger and better than before. You'll see.
Lydia (*after a pause*) All right Alec, I'll take your word for it. Millions wouldn't.

Alec chuckles

If you're really on the level I'll do what I can to help. I hope you pull it off.
Alec Twelve months from now he'll thank me with tears in his eyes and we'll all be living at the Ritz. In the meantime what he doesn't know won't hurt him. It's going to be a big year for Herbert. What did you think of the old joker's will? Do you suppose Herbert could learn to play first instead of second fiddle?
Lydia You're a fine one to talk about fiddles. I feel very sorry for that poor little man. He brings out all my latent maternal instincts. Tell me, Alec, why am I such a pushover for anything weak and helpless?
Alec (*grinning*) Your trouble is you're allergic to he-men. That's why ours has been such a strictly business relationship all these years.

Herbert appears in a dressing-gown at the top of the stairs

Alec Five carbons Miss Prentice and tell Sean Connery we're fully cast at the moment but we'll bear him in mind in case we have anything for him later on. Thank Bernard Levin for his greetings telegram and tell the Film Critics Benevolent Fund I'm sending them a cheque for a thousand pounds. Ah, Herbert!
Lydia Will that be all, Mr Ogleby?
Alec That's all for the moment, Miss Prentice.

Act II, Scene 1 29

Lydia Good night, Mr Ogleby. Goodnight Herbert. Keep your wits about you.

Lydia exits upstairs

Alec Now, let me see, where were we? Ah, yes, Wardour Street. That's where the money is. And where money is money will be. Of course there's a lot of people who think they're sitting pretty.

He pushes Herbert down into the chair above the table

They think they've only got to be nice to old Ogleby and they're in. Not so easy old boy. I'm too fly. Open-handed Ogleby may be, but not empty-headed. (*He hands Herbert a cigar*) But never let it be said that I left an old school chum out in the cold when I could have let him in on the ground floor. Here's the situation in a nutshell. (*He cracks a walnut*) What would you say to a business investment that enabled you to have your cake and eat it too? That brought you in an approximate annual return equivalent to the aggregate sum total of your original capital investment and yet keep your initial capital holding intact?
Herbert I beg your pardon?
Alec I'm floating a new company. Phoenix Films. Competition in the City is so fierce, so many investors are anxious to buy up shares that I'm simply selecting a few old friends, like yourself, and quietly doing them a good turn for old times' sake.
Herbert But I ...
Alec We go on location in March. Six weeks on the Neapolitan Riviera. Sorrento, Amalfi, Positano. "It happened in Amalfi."
Herbert What did?
Alec That's the title of the film. Then we come back to England for the studio work. It'll be the film of the year. I've got a tie-up with Amalgamated Exhibitors, I'm affiliated to the Motion Picture Preview Association of America and I'm hand in glove with the Cinematograph Distribution Group. We'll have it dubbed for the Middle West and strictly between ourselves I've already arranged for it to receive an Oscar. Just let me have your cheque for two hundred thousand ... tomorrow will do ... and then I'll put you on the board of directors and all you have to do is sit back and wait for the profits to roll in when the film is shown.
Herbert I don't know what to say. I haven't got two hundred thousand pounds. I've only a yearly allowance and anyway ...
Alec Look, old boy. Any bank will advance you two hundred thousand against your expectations. Leave it to me, I'll get my solicitors to fix the business details for you. We won't bother old ... what's his name ... Gosforth. He wouldn't understand the way we arrange these things in the film industry. (*He shakes Herbert's hand energetically*) You're a lucky man Herbert! You've not only come into a packet of money but with me to open the door for you you've snapped up a golden opportunity that's going to turn your little packet into a great big parcel! Congratulations, old boy.

Gripe enters DL *with a tray to collect glasses*

Herbert But ...

Alec That's all right, don't thank me. You can leave it all to me. Now then Cripps, find us a couple of fresh glasses. We'll have a drink to seal the bargain. (*He regards a depleted port bottle*) Wait a minute. This calls for something more exciting than port.

Bunny appears at the top of the stairs wearing Belinda's pyjamas, which are rather large for her

I've got a bottle of bubbly in the back of the car. (*He moves to the door*) I'll be back in a minute and then we'll drink a toast to Herbert Budgett of Phoenix Films. No, no don't please don't thank me. I'm only too glad to have had the opportunity of extending a helping hand to an old schoolfellow. You remember the motto of the old school ... "Do while you can and having done depart."

Alec exits

Gripe Have you been foolish?

Gripe exits DL

Bunny Mr Budgett! Did he say Phoenix Films?

Herbert (*rising*) Yes, that's right. He did.

Bunny Does he want you to lend him money and is he going to put you on his board of directors?

Herbert Yes. How did you know?

Bunny You won't let him will you?

Herbert Well, I suppose I might. He seems to think ...

Bunny Oh, you mustn't! Mr Hackenschmidt wouldn't!

Herbert Mr Hackenschmidt?

Bunny He's got quite a lot of money but he wouldn't let Mr Ogleby have any. I heard them quarrelling about it. Mr Hackenschmidt said it would only be throwing good money after bad.

Herbert The proprietor of the circus? He said that to Ogleby? But why? When?

Bunny It was only this afternoon, see, and they were arguing. It seems that this Mr Ogleby isn't exactly what you might call truthful. I wouldn't say he was actually crooked but he isn't altogether straight. I heard all the ins and outs of it from Mavis. She's one of our equestrians, she rides barebacked. Well, she's a very intimate friend of Mr Hackenschmidt, if you know what I mean, and she heard all about it from him. Felix Films ... that was the name all right. Apparently this Ogleby had had a lot of money from him some time ago to make this film but Ogleby only used it to pay off somebody else he owed money to. And now Mr Hackenschmidt says he won't give him any more and he's going to put the police on to him unless he pays him back. I knew I'd seen his face before somewhere and now I know where it was. It was coming out of Mr Hackenschmidt's caravan after they'd had the row. He got into his car with that secretary of his and off they went, plunged in thought. I do hope you don't think I'm a busybody but I felt you ought to know.

Act II, Scene 1

Herbert I'm very grateful to you. It looks as if you've saved me from losing a large sum of money. It's very kind of you to take the trouble to warn me.
Bunny Oh, that's quite all right. It was lucky I came in just in time to catch what he said. As a matter of fact I really came down to tell you how much I appreciated all you've done and to say "Toodle-oo". I'm off first thing in the morning.
Herbert You're going?
Bunny Oh yes, I must.
Herbert But is that wise? I thought we'd agreed that you would stay here until the coast was clear. You can't go back and let that ruffian throw knives at you all over again. You *can't* go back to the circus. *You mustn't!*
Bunny What else can I do? A girl must live.
Herbert Couldn't you go home to your parents?
Bunny They both died when I was very young.
Herbert Wasn't there anyone to look after you?
Bunny There was an uncle but he's dead now and he was quite horrid at the time. He sent me to an orphanage but I was very unhappy there so one day I ran away.
Herbert Oh, you poor little woman! How did you come to be with the circus?
Bunny Well you see, I went on the stage when I was twelve. I started as a fairy in Walsall. *Jack and the Beanstalk.* Oh, I've been around.
Herbert I'm worried about you.
Bunny That's sweet of you. But don't you worry. I can take care of myself all right.
Herbert But you shouldn't have to. You need someone to ... to ... (*He hesitates*)
Bunny (softly) I think I'd better say goodnight now, Mr Budgett.
Herbert No ... wait ... Miss ... Isn't it silly. I can't even remember your name.
Bunny Tucker. Millie Tucker. But my friends call me Bunny. You can call me Bunny.
Herbert Does that mean I'm a friend?
Bunny Oh yes, of course! I liked you the moment I saw you. I knew you were somebody I could trust. There aren't many men I could say that about.
Herbert I don't know what to say.
Bunny That's one of the things I like about you. Lots of other men would have said something clever or something nice they didn't really mean but you're too honest for that.

There is a pause

   (*Gently*) Goodbye. Thanks for everything.

   Bunny exits upstairs

Church bells are heard in the far distance muffled by the falling snow

Herbert, left alone, stands looking after Bunny for a moment. He moves slowly to the table and sits, in the chair above it. Then he quietly covers his face with his hands

Gripe enters DL *with a large pewter tankard of Creeching claret*

Gripe There we are, sir. One pint tankard ruby red. A drink fit for the Devil himself. It's made by a secret process known only to myself. The grapes are grown in a special place and must be trodden at midnight. It used to be made by the monks in the old monastery of Creeching Priors. They had some times there, I can tell you! . . . Until the Abbot got struck by lightning. There's more in these things than meets the eye. Go on. It'll do wonders for you.

Urged by Gripe, Herbert tentatively sips the claret. He finds it so much to his liking that the tankard is soon half empty

Can you feel it running up and down your veins like red 'ot maggots?
Herbert (*half rising*) It certainly is warming.
Gripe Can you feel it tingling in your toes and loosening your eyes in their sockets?
Herbert Most extraordinary. I wouldn't have believed it!
Gripe Can you feel yourself blossoming like a rose in midsummer and smoking like a muck heap in the sun?

The bells stop

Herbert (*pushing back his chair and drawing himself up full length*) By Jove! I believe I can!
Gripe (*off hand*) Not a bad drink is it?

Alec enters with a bottle of champagne

Alec (*as he removes the cork with a loud pop*) What's that you've got? The local hell-broth? Old Granny Gripe's brew?

The bells begin again

Hark! The Christmas bells! Noël! Wassail! (*He pours out three glasses of champagne*) Here you are, Gripe. The skin off your nose. A merry Christmas to us each and every one. To the future of Phoenix Films! How about you Gripe? Haven't you got a toast?
Gripe (*raising his glass*) To the spirits of Christmas past. And may we all sleep quiet in our own beds. (*He sniggers*)
Alec You dirty old rascal. What about you Herbert?
Herbert (*more than a little flushed*) "To our sweethearts and wives. May they never meet."
Alathea (*off; distant*) Herbert!

Herbert drains his glass before he speaks

Herbert (*quietly and deliberately*) All right . . . my dear . . . I'm coming.

Herbert moves towards the stairs as

The CURTAIN *falls*

Scene 2

Later that night

The stage is empty, lit only by moonlight shining in through the leaded windows and by the flickering firelight which is causing weird shadows to dance on the walls

A grandfather clock off right chimes once

There is a ghostly rattling of chains and a peal of mad laughter in the distance

Cyril appears in a flamboyant dressing-gown at the top of the stairs. He comes downstairs and exits to the kitchen

Thundercloud enters UR, *crosses the stage and exits up the stairs*

Cyril enters with three bottles of Creeching Claret which are covered in cobwebs. He puts them on the table, then moves to the coat rack for his cigarette case and lighter which are in his overcoat pocket. He is making an ineffectual attempt to get the lighter to work when the panel behind him opens abruptly and a naked, blood-stained grey arm makes a sudden grab, reaching out to seize the unsuspecting Cyril by the throat. His back turned, he is only just out of reach of the agitated, clutching fingers which, after two or three unavailing attempts, give up, and the panel closes. Cyril manages to light a cigarette and returns to the table. He removes cobwebs from the bottle

Alec enters from upstairs

Alec Psst!
Cyril (*almost jumping out of his skin*) My God! Oh, it's you. Thank Heaven.
Alec (*switching on the main lights*) Who did you think it was?
Cyril This place gives me the jim-jams. It makes my goose flesh. In my room there's a cupboard six feet tall.
Alec What about it?
Cyril It's locked and it creaks. I couldn't get off so I got up and came down ... for a glass of water.
Alec (*picking up one of the bottles*) So I see.
Cyril According to Gripe this is pretty hot stuff. Rightly famed.
Alec I've always put claret in the same category as barley wine and tonic water. What's so special about this I wonder? Come on, we'll put it to the test.
Cyril Here's a corkscrew.

Alec starts to open a bottle

What are you doing up ... I mean down? Couldn't you sleep either?
Alec Not after that supper Gripe gave us. I feel as if there's a pound of pebbles in my stomach. I didn't care for those black puddings either. Mine was full of dog's claws.

Cyril is staring into the fire and Alec is busy with the corkscrew as:

The Ghost of Montague Cheyney enters UL—*a horrible and mouldy figure, decayed at the edges, and wearing doublet and hose and an Elizabethan ruff.*

(Note: This being a REAL ghost, do not use a mask. Rely instead on an imaginative make-up!) The Ghost descends the stairs unnoticed, the kitchen door opens mysteriously before he reaches it and he exits DL

Alec *(extracting the cork)* All we need now are some glasses. There should be some in the kitchen.

Alec exits DL and returns almost at once with two glasses. He shivers

Brr! Damn cold in that kitchen. Icy. There's a horrible smell in there too. *(He pours out two glasses of claret)* Must be something mouldering under the floor. I don't know what it is but it's been dead a damn long time. *(He hands a glass of claret to Cyril)* What are you looking so glum about?
Cyril I was thinking about women. How queer they are.
Alec Speak as you find, of course. Personally I've always . . .
Cyril I mean their whims.
Alec Eh?
Cyril They're so fickle. So untrustworthy. You never know where you are with a woman. Look at Belinda.
Alec I have and very nice too.
Cyril There was nothing official but it was an understood thing. Then she comes into all this money and casts me aside. She said I was only a wild oat.
Alec Don't take it to heart old boy. There's many a pebble lying on the foreshore, just waiting to be picked up.
Cyril But they're not all like Belinda.
Alec They haven't all got sixty thousand a year, that's perfectly true. But you be guided by your Uncle Alec. If you want to get a woman really interested in you then start making eyes at somebody else. It never fails.
Cyril Do you really think so?
Alec Of course, some of them turn a bit nasty. You might get your face scratched. I say, this stuff's all right isn't it? I've never known claret taste like this before! *(He replenishes both glasses)* The thing to remember is that a young woman is a creature of the jungle. *(He perches on the downstage end of the table, his feet dangling just above the floor)* We are civilized. *They're* not. Do you know the difference between a man and a woman?
Cyril Well, yes of course. Why, I remember when I was only fifteen . . .
Alec No . . . No old boy. I'm not talking about the physical fundamentals. You can tell me the tale of the tobacconist's daughter some other time.

The Ghost enters DL and stands by the table staring at Alec

(Shivering) Put another log on the fire, it's getting damn chilly in here now. A man has good solid reasons for everything he does . . .

The Ghost moves behind Alec and to his R

Half a tick, I'll open another bottle.

Occupied once again with the corkscrew Alec is unaware that The Ghost moves down and stands beside Cyril who is still staring into the fire

Act II, Scene 2   35

Women are an entirely different proposition. Their every action is motivated by the desire to get the better of some poor devil in trousers. (*He sniffs the air around him*) Well I'm damned. That mouldy smell's in here now. Give us your glass, Cyril. (*Without looking round he holds out his hand towards Cyril*)

The Ghost takes the glass from Cyril and hands it to Alec who fills it and passes it back along the same route

The Ghost exits UR

Alec Cheers.
Cyril Cheers.
Alec Women are a damned nuisance but, mind you, they have their points. Especially your Belinda. The moment I clapped eyes on Belinda ...
Cyril (*draining his glass, rising and moving left to behind the table*) Yes, I noticed you doing that.
Alec I said to myself, "Alec", I said ... that's my name ... I said, "This young woman has possibilities."
Cyril (*refilling the glasses*) I bet you did. Have another drink ... down the hatch.
Alec Bob's your uncle.

They clink their glasses together and drink

Cyril You really think I could make Belinda jealous if I tried?
Alec You'd have to do the thing thoroughly of course. No half measures. 'Strewth! What do they put in this stuff! (*He tops up the glasses*)
Cyril I feel strangely exhilarated.
Alec (*in alarm*) Look! I can't get my feet to touch the ground!
Cyril It must be the carpet. It isn't quite on the floor. (*He treads the carpet down firmly and addresses it sternly*) Get down will you! And stay down!
Alec (*beckoning to Cyril*) Tell me something. I don't want to pry, but why have you got four ears? (*He stares closely into Cyril's face*) Good Lord!
Cyril What's the matter now?
Alec You've got two noses, too ... Do they run in the family?
Cyril Your face. My God, your face!
Alec What about it?
Cyril It keeps getting larger and smaller ... (*his hands indicate the process*) ... larger and smaller ... larger and smaller ... larger and ...
Alec Stop playing that blasted concertina ... You'll wake everybody up. Let's change the subject. What shall we talk about?
Cyril I don't mind. Anything you like. Women if you like.
Alec Ah, women. There's a fruitful topject... subjic. I'll tell you about women. They're a biological necessity.
Cyril A birological necessity.
Alec But we've got to keep them in their place. Once they get the whip hand there's no doing anything with them. You take Alathea.
Cyril I'd rather not. You take her.
Alec Let's have a drink instead. (*He refills the glasses, resting the bottle on his shoulder as if it were a wine-skin*) First today.

Cyril (*starting to sing*) "Good King Wencelas looked out, Deep and crisp and Stephen."
Alec Just a moment. Simply because you've had a few there's no need to make spectacles of yourselves.
Cyril (*contritely*) Sorry. I forgot myself.

There is a pause

Cyril I don't usually.
Alec What?
Cyril Pardon?
Alec Don't what?

Cyril looks blank

You said "I don't usually".
Cyril Well, if it comes to that *I* don't either. Let's have another drink.
Alec (*breaking into song*) "Gin, gin, was mother's ruin . . ."
Cyril ⎱ (*together*) "Mother's ruin will be mine.
Alec ⎰ Poor Auntie Jane was a prey to champagne."

Belinda appears at the top of the stairs

Cyril ⎱ (*together*) "Father preferred turpentine . . ."
Alec ⎰
Belinda You boys are certainly full of the Christmas spirit.
Alec (*moving to the stairs*) Ah, this is better. There's nothing like a little feminine companionship in the small hours.

Alec takes Belinda's hand and leads her down the stairs, eyeing her admiringly

You look very fetching if I may say so. If I were a ghost I wouldn't bother to haunt anybody else's room tonight. I'd concentrate on yours.
Belinda In that case I'm glad you're flesh and blood, Mr Ogleby.
Alec Are you really? Call me Alec. Why, you're quite chilly, you poor little girl. Let me warm your frozen flesh. (*He rubs her arms and back*)
Belinda Oh, that's nice . . . Ooh, lovely!
Alec Are you beginning to tingle? I'll do the front when we're alone.

Alec leads Belinda towards the fireplace and pulls the settee round so that it faces the fire

Come and toast your toes.

Alec winks at Cyril over Belinda's shoulder and joins her in the depths of the settee

Cyril has observed this easy conquest with astonishment and envy

Lydia enters

Lydia (*descending the stairs*) Will somebody save my life and give me a drink. I'm frozen to the marrow.
Cyril Here you are. Have a glass of Creech.

Cyril glances towards the settee but all he can see of Alec and Belinda is the

Act II, Scene 2   37

backs of their heads. Belinda's head rests on Alec's shoulder and they are whispering together

Why you poor little girl, you are cold! Er ... let me warm my frozen fingers on your flesh. (*He turns Lydia about*)
Lydia I beg your pardon ... ?
Cyril (*rubbing her back heartily*) Is that nice?
Lydia Well ...
Cyril (*for Belinda's benefit*) I'll do the front when we're alone.
Lydia Eh? ... Oh you will, will you?
Cyril Oh yes. And I'll toast your toes too.
Lydia Well, don't exhaust yourself. There's no need to be quite so energetic. No, don't stop just when my circulation's coming back. A bit lower down please, and with more of a circular movement. What are you and Alec doing down here? Couldn't you sleep?
Cyril We've been enjoying an intellectual discussion.
Lydia Well fancy! What about?
Cyril (*airily*) All sorts of things. Women and things. I was just saying to Alec that women are a biological necessity.
Lydia (*after a pause*) I see.

Cyril continues to warm her back absent-mindedly

Mmm! ... Mmmmm! ... Oh yes, I like this.

Lydia slowly turns to face him. Cyril's arms are about her waist

You're a fast worker, aren't you?
Cyril Am I?
Lydia (*very close to him*) You certainly are. I feel quite warm.
Cyril Yes. (*He swallows*) I know.
Lydia Christmas Day at Creeching Cheyney has possibilities after all.
Cyril Has it?
Lydia (*softly*) Oh yes.

Her arms go around his neck and they kiss lingeringly

During the prolonged kiss the panel opens to reveal a ghastly chalk-white face with blood-red lips, which stares at them in amazement. The panel closes

Lydia I feel better already. (*She disengages herself*) Now how about that drink? (*She drains Cyril's glass*)
Belinda (*laughing, as she rises from the settee*) I don't believe a word of it. I think you're just tiddley.
Alec (*rising to his feet*) No, it's perfectly true.
Belinda Hello, you two. (*She holds up a bottle from the table*) What's this like?
Alec (*moving to the table*) Quite a bit warmer down here now, isn't it? (*He pours a drink into his glass for Belinda*)
Cyril Quite a bit.

Lydia leads Cyril by the hand and settles down into the settee with him

Alec The moment I saw you I thought to myself . . . well, that's neither here nor there.
Belinda Go on. I'm interested.
Alec Well, it's like this. In the film business one sees all sorts of women. But under the surface they're all very much the same. Ah, the monotony of it all! Yet once in a while one finds a women who is subtly different from the common herd.
Belinda If that's meant to be a compliment it's a very clumsy one. I'm sure you can do better than that.
Alec What I'm trying to say is that you have a certain something the others haven't got.
Belinda Yes. Thanks to Uncle Desmond's will. Tell me more about this new film. When do you start production?
Alec All right.

Alec sits in the large armchair and pulls her down on to his lap

Snuggle up close to Uncle Alec and keep the cold out.

Belinda does so

What a good thing you came down. I hate to think of you lying up there in your great bed of Ware, lonely and frightened. With nobody by your side to protect you.

Alathea enters from the stairs

Alathea Belinda! What are you doing?
Belinda Don't worry Mother. I just came down for a glass of water.
Alathea Come along, Herbert. Don't dawdle.
Belinda About this film of yours. What's it called?
Alathea Herbert! Who is that you're talking to?
Herbert (*off*) It's all right my dear. It's Miss Tucker. She couldn't find the switch.
Alathea Which switch?
Herbert (*as he appears at the top of the stairs*) The one in the corridor.

Bunny enters from the stairs

Her bedroom is at the far end.
Alathea Indeed.
Bunny Mr Budgett very kindly gave me a helping hand in the dark.
Alathea Oh he did?

Lydia and Cyril rise from the settee

Lydia What brings you down Mrs Budgett? Couldn't you sleep either?
Alathea I was kept awake by the wind.
Alec It must have been those pickled onions. (*He raises his glass*) Have a drop of this. It'll straighten you out in no time.
Alathea (*crossing to the fire*) Certainly not.
Alec What about you Herbert? (*To Cyril*) I suppose he came down for a glass of water, eh?

Act II, Scene 2   39

Herbert Why no. (*He joins Alathea by the fire*) As a matter of fact I felt like a biscuit.
Alathea (*to Bunny*) What were you doing, wandering about the house at this time of night?
Bunny Well, I was just going off in the arms of Orpheus when I heard something scratching outside my door. I couldn't lie in bed just wondering what it was, so I got up.
Lydia What was it?
Bunny I opened my door and got the fright of my life. It was hanging upside down on the doorknob.
Cyril What was?
Bunny A bat. One of Gripe's bats.
Lydia Oh no!

There are general noises of repugnance

Bunny It rustled its wings at me. I think it's going to spend the night there.
Lydia There was a rustling noise under my bed. Do you suppose that was bats too!
Herbert It's quite probable. The house is infested with them. Gripe tells me they breed in the attic.
Cyril What a nasty thought.
Herbert It's all because of the seventeenth-century roof. They nest in the thatch.
Bunny It gave me ever such a turn, I can tell you.
Lydia I don't know about you, but I'm not going upstairs again until somebody has looked under my bed and chased the horrid things away.
Cyril (*looking at Alec*) There's a nice job for somebody. I know the very man.
Alec That's jolly sporting of you Cyril. I was going to offer myself but since you've beaten me to it . . .
Cyril (*horrified*) What! No . . . no!
Alec Since you were the first to volunteer . . .
Cyril Now wait a minute.
Alec . . . it's only fair that you should have the fun.
Lydia Oh, would you really do that for me?
Alec Of course he would. Wouldn't you?
Lydia I think you're so brave.
Cyril (*looking deep into her eyes*) Am I? Oh well, in that case . . .
Alec (*taking Gosforth's bowler hat from the stand*) You'd better wear this.
Cyril What for?
Alec You heard what he said. They nest in the thatch. Go on. (*He places the hat firmly on Cyril's head*) Up you go.
Cyril Wouldn't you like to come too?
Alec (*propelling him up the stairs*) Go on. Show the stuff you're made of. (*He hands Cyril an umbrella*) Here. You can jab at them with this. It's the easiest job in the world, just getting rid of a few bats.
Cyril (*indignantly*) Oh, is it? Suppose you try.

Alec If they attack you the idea is to open that and get underneath it. Off you go.

Cyril stands unhappily at the top of the stairs

Cyril (*to Lydia*) See you later ... I hope.

Cyril exits

Alec He'll be all right. Making such a fuss about a little thing like that.
Lydia I don't think he made a fuss at all. I notice you wouldn't go.
Alec I wanted him to have all the credit.
Bunny I hope he doesn't meet any ghosts.
Lydia That's all we need. If Cyril comes back and reports there's a ghost on the upstairs landing, I'm staying down here till the morning.
Belinda Me too. I don't mind having my blood sucked by bats. That's obviously going to be part of the nightly routine for the next twelve months. But I do draw the line at phantoms.
Lydia It might be rather fun. We could keep the fire going and share these coats between us.

Herbert moves to the coat rack

I'm sure Cyril would keep me warm till daylight.
Alec Is there a young and preferably unattached female with whom I could share this travelling rug?
Belinda Right here, darling. If ever a girl needed a man's protection, tonight's the night.

Alec drapes his travelling rug around her shoulders

Herbert (*seeing Bunny shivering*) Don't catch cold. You'd better put this on. (*He puts his overcoat around her*)
Alathea Herbert! Come over here at once.
Belinda Poor old Cyril. I expect he's having kittens by now.

Cyril's head appears at the top of the stairs

Cyril They don't bite, do they?
Alec Haven't you gone yet?
Cyril No. Not yet. I thought I saw something lurking along the corridor.
Alec Go on. Be a man.
Cyril (*aggrieved*) All right. You needn't be so petulant. I'm going.

Cyril exits. Immediately there is the twang of a bowstring and a yell from Cyril who re-appears, a large arrow through his bowler

Help! I've been transfixed! (*He hurries down the stairs*)
Lydia What is it. What happened?
Alec Where did you get that from?
Cyril I don't know! It came out of the dark!
Bunny Thundercloud!
Alec Who?

Act II, Scene 2

Bunny He said he'd come back! He can put an arrow through an apple at forty paces!

Herbert You mean he's in the house now!

The lights go out and there is a terrifying scream from off left

There is general commotion and shouts of "Good God, what was that?" "What's happening?" "Who turned the lights off?" etc

> *Thundercloud rushes on at the top of the stairs, his bow still in his hand. He pauses for a moment in the moonlight coming through the small leaded window and looks back along the corridor in horror. What he sees causes him to run gibbering down the stairs and out through the main door*

Alec What was all that about? AAAHH!

> *All shrink back in terror and the women shriek as an apparition appears at the top of the stairs. This is NOT the Ghost of Montague Cheyney. Nor is it one of the lesser spectres which have been glimpsed earlier making homicidal overtures from behind a panel. DO use a Guy Fawkes type mask for this one, with a black slouch hat from beneath which trail long whisps of grey hair. The figure is wrapped in a long grey cloak*

As it appears, a green spot, concealed halfway down the stairs, shines upon its face. It lifts its arms and rolls its head horribly

Meanwhile there is pandemonium downstairs, everybody bumping into everybody else, falling over the furniture, etc, to the accompaniment of cries of "Look out! It's coming down!" "Get off my foot" etc.

> *The apparition glides away as silently as it appeared*

> *Gripe enters from the kitchen. He is wearing a white nightshirt and nightcap and carrying a branched candlestick. He grins at them over the flickering candles*

Gripe Merry Christmas everybody!

Quick CURTAIN

ACT III

Christmas Day

A BBC Male Voice Choir is heard singing, somewhat ominously, "God Rest Ye Merry Gentlemen, Let Nothing You Dismay."

After a moment the CURTAIN *rises to reveal Alec and Cyril listening disconsolately to a transistor radio which stands on the table*

Alec is seated right of the table, his elbow resting upon it and his chin cupped in his left hand. Cyril is in exactly the corresponding position left of the table. The gentlemen are looking anything but merry ... although both are wearing gay paper hats. The walls are hung with Xmas decorations, holly and mistletoe. A small but well-bedecked Christmas tree stands on a small table in front of the window. The curtains are apart but the windows are obscured from the outside by snow. The lights are on and the settee has been moved back to its original position

Radio announcer We interrupt this programme of carols to give you a weather report. A deep depression has settled over the British Isles. Snow continues to fall in all parts.

The wind howls off

A blizzard is raging in the Western counties where many country districts are completely cut off. Several villages are buried beneath the snow. Telephone wires are down and motor traffic is at a standstill. A cyclone is approaching from the North Atlantic ...

Alec switches off the radio

Alec Trapped.
Cyril Cut off.

Lydia enters DL, *carrying a spade*

Alec We shall be here for days yet.
Cyril We shall just have to resign ourselves.
Lydia (*briskly*) That's not the right attitude. There's work to be done. If we're all going to spend the night down here again we shall need some more wood for the fire. Come along Cyril, pull your socks up. You'll find a chopper and a tree trunk outside the back door.
Cyril (*meekly*) Yes, darling. (*He pulls up his socks*)

Cyril exits DL

Lydia Now then, Alec. Shake a leg.

Act III

Alec winces and shakes a leg

Your car's almost buried under the snow again. Take this spade and dig it out.

Alec What's the use? I can't get it to go with the radiator full of ice.

Lydia Never mind about that. The important thing is to keep busy.

Alec Why?

Lydia With the 'phone out of order and both the cars immobilized it may be a week before we can get through to the village on foot.

Cyril enters, chopper in hand. He moves to the umbrella stand for his overcoat

We must look upon ourselves as castaways, thrown back on our own resources.

Alec You're getting quite a kick out of this aren't you?

Lydia We must face up to the fact that we're in a very serious situation, half buried in the snow, with food running short and things that go bump in the night all around us.

Cyril Oh don't. It makes my blood run hot and cold just to think about it. I'll never forget last night.

Lydia (*a soft gleam in her eyes*) Neither shall I.

Alec The floor was hard but the company was congenial. (*He winks at Cyril*) Eh, Cyril?

Lydia Off you go, Alec. A little healthy outdoor exercise will do you good.

Alec Now look here ... Oh, I see. (*He moves to the main door*) Look out, Cyril. She's after you.

Alec exits

Cyril moves towards the kitchen

Lydia Don't go Cyril. Kiss me. (*She puts her arms around his neck and kisses him violently*) Oh darling, it's so wonderful to be alone together. There's so much of me that's been lying dormant, just waiting for you to come along. Ever since you swept me off my feet I don't know whether I'm on my head or my heels.

Cyril (*overwhelmed*) D ... Darling.

Lydia You bring out all that's maternal in me.

Cyril (*weakly*) Do I, darling?

Lydia I want to be a mother, a sister and a mistress to you. I want to fill your life to the brim.

Cyril That's very decent of you.

Lydia You know what you've done to me don't you? You've taken my susceptible woman's heart in your strong masculine hands ... you've transformed me from a brittle shallow person into a creature all feminine, all woman ... all yours! Kiss me again.

Lydia kisses him with passionate abandon. Cyril is bent backwards across the table

Oh darling, I'm just like clay in your arms. You do love me, don't you?

Cyril Oh yes, I do. I think you're wonderful. I've never known a woman like you.
Lydia When I'm with you I feel as if I'm in the grip of some mighty force.
Cyril (*still semi-recumbent*) That's just how I feel too. Excuse me. (*He removes the chopper from the small of his back and straightens up*)
Lydia (*nestling against him*) When I look at you my heart goes pitter-patter ... pitter-patter ... How does yours go?
Cyril Mine goes patter-pitter ... patter-pitter ...
Lydia Last night as we lay together, in front of the fire, I found myself feeling weak and defenceless ... I tried to keep calm ... I tried to be strong and matter-of-fact ... but I knew something was happening to me that had never happened before.
Cyril Me too.
Lydia There were bells ringing in the depths of my feminine being.
Cyril Good Lord! I did all that to you?
Lydia Darling, you do it all the time, whenever I'm near you.
Cyril (*delighted*) Do I really? I've never had that effect on a woman before. To be perfectly frank with you, most women think I'm a bit of a drip.
Lydia (*caressing his cheek*) Sweet Cyril.
Cyril I'm not very bright, you know. What I mean is, I'm not very good at thinking things out.
Lydia Don't worry darling, I'll think for both of us. Just you be your sweet adorable self.
Cyril All right darling. I'll try. You're very good for me. I feel a new man. (*He twirls the chopper carelessly*) Well, I'll just go out and lop off a few logs.

Gripe enters UL

'Bye darling.
Lydia Sweetheart.

With a cheery wave of the chopper Cyril exits DL

Gripe (*slyly*) Is there anything else you require, Miss?
Lydia Let me see. (*She looks round the room*) No, I don't think so, Gripe. The tree looks very fine now. You had the right idea there. It's amazing how a few Christmas decorations have helped to calm down the nervy ones. I've done my best to keep them all busy and prevent them from becoming hysterical as it gets darker. Do you think we'll see it again tonight?
Gripe There's none can tell. Strange things happen in this house. There's something evil hovering ... in the air around us (*looking around apprehensively*) waiting to pounce ...
Lydia Oh don't! You make my flesh creep.
Gripe There's terrible things been done within these walls in days gone by. Suicide, patricide, fraticide, homicide ... insecticide ... the lot. It's left a nasty stain on the place.
Lydia I don't envy the Budgetts having to stay here for a whole year.

Act III   45

Gripe Twelve months is a long time. Much might happen before next Christmas. They may not last that long.
Lydia How long will it be before we can struggle through to the village on foot?
Gripe (*enigmatically*) Who can look into the seeds of time and say which ones will grow?
Lydia Well, will it snow again tonight, do you think?
Gripe (*moving* UR) I'll go and tap on the late master's barometer. If that says fair ... then there's more snow on the way.

Gripe exits UR

Lydia (*following him*) I'll come with you. If there's a chance of the weather clearing up I'd like to know about it.

Lydia exits UR

Cyril enters DL *with the chopper, having sliced the top off his thumb*

Cyril (*in distress as he enters*) Darling, I'm injured ... (*he realises the room is empty*) Oh ... (*he woefully regards his bloodstained thumb*. Having no handkerchief himself, he goes to the coat stand and takes one from the breast pocket of Gosforth's overcoat*)

Cyril is bandaging his thumb with difficulty when the panel opens very slowly, inch by inch, to reveal a horrible staring face, framed in black velvet

Alec enters UC *carrying the spade and finishing a cigarette*

The panel closes

Alec What are you up to? I thought you were chopping wood?
Cyril I was, but I chopped myself in error. If it comes to that I thought you were clearing snow away.
Alec No fear. (*He stands the spade by the door*) You won't catch me floundering about out there. It's four feet deep in places and there's a thick white mist over everything. (*He stubs out his cigarette*) I've been having a quiet smoke under the porch. Here, let me do that for you. (*He assists Cyril*)
Cyril I wonder where Lydia is?
Alec I don't know what's come over that girl. She's padding about like a panther with its young. You can almost see her swish her tail.
Cyril (*huffily*) I don't agree. I think she's marvellous.
Alec I didn't say she wasn't, but I hope you know what you're doing.
Cyril I'm fully capable thank you. You poke your nose into your own affairs.
Alec All right, keep your shirt on. I'm only giving you a word of warning. She never used to be like this. Efficient, yes, but always unobtrusive. The perfect secretary. Discreet. Impersonal.
Cyril I think she's terrific. She reminds me of some exotic flower ... dark ... proud ... fierce ... beautiful.
Alec Oh my gawd!

Cyril It's not a thing to mock at.
Alec You know Cyril, women are funny creatures. It's a good thing I understand them. Always going out of their way to prove to men how adorably feminine they are. Adorably feminine, my Aunt Fanny.
Cyril There's no need to be blasphemous.
Alec Sweet as pie one minute and scratch your eyes out the next. Look at Delilah. Look what she did to Samson. Look at Lady Macbeth. Look at Lot's wife. Turned her husband into a pillar of salt. Not for me the marriage tie. I'd as soon throw myself in the river.
Cyril Sour grapes.
Alec What's that?
Cyril Sour grapes I said and I'll say it again. Sour grapes.
Alec Not in the least. I've nearly been caught more times than I can count but I'm up to all their little tricks and dodges. I know the unscrupulous way they play upon a man's finer feelings and arouse his compassion, his protective instincts, his natural generosity of spirit. (*He chuckles*) Oh yes, they've tried to get a bridle on me quite a few times. But this old trout's too fly to be caught with that bait.
Cyril (*testily*) I wish you'd make up your mind whether you're a horse or a fish.
Alec Now see here, Carraway . . .

Lydia is heard off talking to Gripe

Look out, here she comes.

Alec grabs the spade and exits

Lydia and Gripe enter UR

Lydia (*crossing to Cyril in concern*) Darling! Whatever's happened to your poor hand!
Cyril It wasn't looking what it was doing . . .
Lydia Oh, my poor darling. Come in here and we'll put it under the tap. You must take care of your precious self.
Cyril It's all right. It doesn't . . . really hurt . . . not . . . very . . . much . . . Ugh! . . . Oo!
Lydia You're so brave Cyril. Here, lean on me.

Lydia and Cyril exit DL

Gripe hugs himself with glee. He does a few steps of a Highland Fling and exits UL *shaking with suppressed mirth*

As he goes Bunny and Belinda enter UR

Bunny If we get some blankets and pillows we can make ourselves quite comfortable.
Belinda We'll keep the fire going all night.
Bunny It might be worse. It's a good thing we've got a wireless. We can hear Bob Monkhouse's Christmas Party and cheer ourselves up a bit.
Belinda Personally I'd rather have Gripe and the ghosts.

Act III

Bunny Oh dear! I never thought I'd ever come into contact with the supernatural.

Lydia enters DL

Belinda Hello Lydia. We're going to bring some blankets down before it gets too dark. Are you coming?
Lydia Good idea. Let's hope the ghosts don't walk before midnight.
Bunny Oh, wasn't it dreadful last night! I don't mind telling you I was really rather petrified.
Belinda You had nothing on me, Bunny. I was in a blue funk.
Bunny I wouldn't sleep upstairs, all by myself, not for all the rice in China.
Lydia Never mind Bunny, you'll be all right tonight. There's safety in numbers.
Bunny The Psychic (*She pronounces the* P) Research Society! They're the people we ought to get on to. They come down with dividing rods and poltergeists and all sort of other gadgets. They exercise the ghosts and take the curse off.
Lydia Are you sure you've got that right?
Bunny Oh yes, I remember reading about it in *Woman's Own*.
Belinda That reminds me. Have you seen Alec anywhere?
Lydia I've set him to work shovelling snow. Men are so helpless aren't they?
Belinda Absolutely. No good at all in an emergency. Have you ever seen anything like the way they behaved when that horrible thing appeared at the top of the stairs? Talk about women and children first! I was nearly trampled to death in the rush.
Lydia Darling, let's face it. Men are worthless creatures, but one has to make allowances for them.
Bunny Oh, I think they're quite nice really. Don't you?
Belinda They have their uses of course. The important thing is never to let them get the whip hand.
Bunny I think they're just right as they are.
Lydia You're too generous Bunny. You have a very sweet nature. Mostly they're pompous, pig-headed and full of their own importance.
Belinda Always trying to make themselves look big.
Lydia Trying to prove how masculine they are. So tiresome.
Belinda It's this inferiority complex they have. It makes them show off all the time. And don't they love to be told how clever they are?
Lydia My dear, they absolutely adore it.
Belinda There's no doubt about it. Every man who ever got on in the world had a woman behind him.
Bunny I'm not so sure about that. It seems to me ...
Belinda The fuss they make about their superior male intelligence and yet a clever woman, simply by using her feminine intuition, and one or two other little things, can always get the better of them.
Bunny I've never thought about it like that. I just take people as I find them.
Lydia Of course there are exceptions. (*A dreamy look comes into her eyes as she gazes fondly towards the kitchen*) Once in a while one finds a man who's different ...

Herbert enters UR *unobserved*

... who needs a warm bosom to rest his head on ... who isn't afraid to be himself ...

Bunny I'm sure you both know much more about it than I do, but it's my opinion that men are very nice just as God made them.

Lydia Hello, Mr Budgett.

Bunny (*flustered*) Oh! I didn't mean ...

Belinda Hello Daddy.

Lydia We're going upstairs to fetch some blankets. Would you like us to bring some for you too?

Herbert That's very kind of you. If it's not too much trouble.

Bunny It's no trouble at all.

Lydia Come along then.

Lydia exits, followed by Bunny

Belinda Where's Mother?

Herbert She's deep in conversation with Mr Gosforth.

Lydia (*off*) Come on, Belinda.

Belinda Coming. Is she still in a state?

Herbert I'm afraid so.

Belinda Oh dear. (*She makes a rueful face*)

Belinda exits

Herbert goes to the bookcase and searches a row of volumes with the same bindings. He finds the book he is seeking and sits in the armchair studying the book intently

Alec enters through the main door, his coat collar turned up. He is blowing on his fingers to warm them. When he sees Herbert he brightens up considerably

Alec Ah, there you are, old boy. I was wondering where you'd got to. (*He glances around to make sure they are alone and then produces a document from his inside pocket*) I've filled in your name and address and all the other little details. All you have to do is put your signature at the bottom. (*He unfolds the document and produces a pen*) I'll get Gripe to witness it and then you're a shareholder and a man with a big future in front of you.

Herbert Yes ... Well now ... I've been thinking over the very generous offer you made me and I'm afraid I've decided against it.

Alec You've what?

Herbert Don't think I'm not grateful to you. I am. But I feel ... that is I ...

Alec This is a chance in a million! A gilt-edged investment!

Herbert Yes, of course ...

Alec I'm doing you a good turn. It's a gift.

Herbert Yes, I realize.

Belinda appears at the top of the stairs

Alec You were keen enough when we talked it over last night.

Act III

Herbert That's not quite true, I'm afraid. It was you who did all the talking, although I was willing enough to let myself be persuaded, as usual. It has become a habit of mine over the years. A bad thing (*He rises*) Yes, a very bad thing indeed. (*He moves towards the door* UR)

Alec Flossie, old son, you're being foolish. Out of the kindness of my heart...

Herbert Oh, I know. It was very good of you. But as a matter of fact I have a little project of my own...

Alec But look here old boy...

Herbert If you'll excuse me, Alec, there are things I must think about. Quietly. By myself.

Herbert exits UR

Alec Well, I'll be...

Belinda No, you won't, Alec. Not if I can help it.

Alec How long have you been there?

Belinda (*coming down*) Now listen, big business man. You're up the creek without a paddle and you know it. What's more I know it and I'm prepared to do something about it.

Alec I don't follow your drift.

Belinda Come along Alec. Cards on the table. So Hackenschmidt wouldn't put up any more cash?

Alec How did you know about Hackenschmidt?

Belinda I've been talking to little Miss Tucker, who shares the confidence of one Mavis, who shares the confidence among other things of Hackenschmidt. Your money troubles aren't exactly top secret.

Alec (*after a moment's hesitation*) All right, it's quite true. Unless I can raise some capital I'm sunk.

Belinda And if you can, what then?

Alec (*walking restlessly up and down*) You seem to know the whole story but I want you to believe me when I tell you that if your father signed this agreement he wouldn't regret it. I'm not shooting a line when I say I know how to make good pictures. Unfortunately I'm flat broke. Every penny I had was in the United Film Corporation. When they went smash so did I. But given the chance I can still turn out the film of the year. You wait and see, that's all! Just you wait and see!

Belinda All right Alec. Don't get excited. You shall.

Alec I don't get you.

Belinda Oh, but you will Alec. That's just the point. You will.

Alec What are you driving at?

Belinda If I marry within twelve months I get sixty thousand a year. Correct?

Alec Yes, but what...

Belinda With sixty thousand a year as security I could raise enough to help finance your film. Isn't that so?

Alec You mean that you...?

Belinda So you know what you have to do before you can start production?

Alec What?

Belinda Marry me.
Alec (*blankly*) Eh?
Belinda The sooner the deed is done the quicker we can get at the cash and the faster I become a shareholder.
Alec (*with a gulp*) Marry you!
Belinda Later on I shall plough back our profits and enlarge the whole organization. With me to guide you you'll be right back at the top in no time.
Alec Oh, you'd guide me would you?
Belinda We'll be a famous team. Anna Neagle and Herbert Wilcox. Bergmann and Rossellini ... Budgett and Ogleby.
Alec But you're not a film star.
Belinda That's right Alec. Not yet. You were wrong about one thing. You said you hadn't found the girl to play the star part in your picture. But you have. She's right here, standing beside you and looking up at you with great big trusting eyes.
Alec Do you mean to say ... !
Belinda Yes Alec, I do. I only lend you the money on condition that I play the girl in the film.
Alec It's blackmail!
Belinda Yes darling. It is, isn't it?
Alec (*desperately*) Now wait a minute! ... I'm thinking. This is ridiculous of course, but ... I wonder ... You're a remarkable young woman ... besides being very easy on the eye ...
Belinda Oh good. That's settled then. We've killed two birds with one stone.
Alec Just a moment. I'm not going to be stampeded into anything. (*He is surveying her from all angles*) I daresay you could play the part ... given the right lighting and provided you didn't try to act. The camera can do that for you ... You'd have to do exactly what I told you and not a fraction more. (*He suddenly makes up his mind*) Yes, it could be done. The snag is I don't enjoy being pushed around like this.
Belinda Alec ... darling Alec ... before you say any more I must tell you there's another reason why I'm proposing to you.
Alec What a woman!
Belinda You see darling, it's difficult for a nice girl like me to explain these things, but I get a funny sort of warm feeling in my tummy whenever I look at you.
Alec You do?
Belinda (*softly*) Yes darling, I do.
Alec (*chuckling, he takes her in his arms*) You do eh?
Belinda I think you're a wonderfully attractive man.
Alec (*basking in her admiration*) Well, why didn't you say so in the first place?
Belinda I've got to marry somebody before next Christmas and it might as well be you.
Alec All right now, don't spoil it.
Belinda (*snuggling against him*) Well, you're ever so handy aren't you?

Act III

Besides, it's good business too. You'll save on my salary. That's another reason why it's such a good idea.
Alec Darling, there are two hundred thousand reasons.
Belinda Darling.

They kiss lingeringly

Alathea and Gosforth are heard off UR

Alec Come in here. We'll put this on a business-like basis.

Alec and Belinda exit DL

Alathea and Gosforth enter UR

Gosforth I strongly advise you to discard any thought of successfully contesting the terms of the will.
Alathea But if it could be established that he was out of his mind when that ridiculous clause was inserted ...
Gosforth The only person who would gain in that event would be your husband's aunt, Emily Budgett. I believe she had some ... ahem ... personal acquaintance with the late Mr Cheyney?
Alathea They were engaged to be married years ago, if that's what you mean. But he jilted her and went to Australia. She swore she'd never forgive him.
Gosforth Ah! In that case she may well endeavour to obtain the legacy for herself.

Cyril enters DL

Alathea (*thoughtfully*) There's more in this than appears on the surface. There are strange things happening in this house.
Cyril That's no news. Not after last night.
Alathea I've got it! Of course! Why didn't I think of it before? If we can be frightened away, even if only for one night, who stands to gain most?
Gosforth Good heavens! You mean ...
Alathea Of course! Emily Budgett.
Cyril You don't think that Aunt Emily ...
Alathea I don't know what to think but I'm sure that hers is the hidden hand in this business!

A muffin bell is rung violently off left

Cyril What on earth ...

Gripe enters UL *dressed as Santa Claus, with a sack over his shoulder*

Alathea Who is this!
Gripe Don't you know me? It's me. Mr Gripe. (*He rings the bell loudly and with deafening effect*)

Alec and Belinda enter DL

Alec What's happening?

Belinda Are we on fire now?
Alec (*as he sees Gripe*) Holy Moses!
Belinda Is *that* who it is?

Gripe cackles and rummages in his sack

Alec I do believe it's ... Can it be?

Herbert enters UR, *book in hand, his finger marking the place*

Gripe Come and get your presents. (*To Herbert*) Here's yours.

Lydia enters UL *carrying blankets*

Herbert sits in the chair above the table and begins to untie his package

There's one for everybody. (*To Lydia*) This is yours.

Bunny and Belinda enter UL *carrying blankets and pillows*

Bunny Whatever's happening?
Gripe I thought I'd give you all a pleasant surprise.
Herbert It's very kind of you.
Gripe (*giving presents to Alathea, Belinda, Bunny, Cyril, Gosforth and Alec*) It does my old 'eart good to see everybody enjoying themselves at Christmas time. The season of goodwill. Peace on earth ... Comfort and joy ... (*He wipes a tear from his eye and a drip from his nose*)
Belinda I do believe he's gone all sentimental.
Bunny There, there, Mr Gripe. You mustn't let it upset you.
Gripe (*blowing his nose noisily*) It comes over me sometimes. (*He rings the bell loudly and unexpectedly*) Long live King William! God save Queen Adelaide!
Alec He can't go back as far as all that surely!
Lydia (*to Cyril, as she unwraps a filmy negligee from its box*) Darling, look! Isn't it lovely. What a wonderful present!
Belinda Alec! I've got one too! (*Hers is even more transparent than Lydia's*) Oh, Gripey! You're sweet. You're a naughty old man but you have nice ideas.

Both girls kiss Gripe, much to his delight

Alec (*holding up a pipe*) This is very handsome.

Alathea has a large box of handkerchiefs and Gosforth a box of cigars

Cyril Good Lord! A lighter that works!
Gripe (*a girl on each arm*) I'm feeling young again. My blood's beginning to tingle. This takes me back to the old days at the Oxford Music Hall. (*He squeezes Belinda*) Supper after the show. (*He squeezes Lydia*) Private rooms. (*He cackles*) Them was the days.
Lydia You wicked old thing. Isn't he terrible!
Herbert (*unwrapping a silver brandy flask*) This is incredibly kind of you. I don't know what to say.
Bunny What a lovely box of chocs! Really you shouldn't have. But it's ever so nice of you.

Act III

Gripe Not half as nice as you deserve, my little dabchick.
Bunny Oh do look! All wrapped in gold and silver paper.
Gripe Chocolates are just like beautiful young women. When you take off their wrappings they're all smooth and sweet.
Bunny Oh, Mr Gripe!
Gripe With lovely soft centres, too.

The three girls laugh, and Gripe hugs them tighter

Alec I don't know what anybody else feels but I suggest we all club together and buy Gripe something really good for a New Year's gift.

There is a general chorus of assent and approval

Lydia Hear, hear!
Cyril I second that.
Belinda It's a jolly good suggestion.
Alec I can't say I exactly took to Gripe the first time I saw him, but it's plain to see he has a heart of gold.
Gripe Oh yes. I grow on people.

There is general laughter as Gripe squeezes the girls again

Alathea (*to Herbert*) What have you got there? What are you sniffing at? (*She takes the flask away from him*)
Herbert It's all right my dear. It's a brandy flask to carry in the pocket. Lots of people have them.
Alathea Do they indeed?
Herbert It's a very useful thing to have on a cold day.
Lydia (*helpfully*) Or on a long train journey.
Belinda (*taking the flask from Alathea*) Why Daddy, it's a beauty. Look it's solid silver.
Herbert It must have cost you a lot of money, I'm afraid. I shall really treasure it.
Alathea You must give it back.

There is a stunned silence

Alec Oh no!
Alathea I've told you before. I will not have you drinking spirits. Give it back at once.
Herbert But my dear, it would be so rude ... It was a gift.
Alathea I'm not going to argue with you. I said give it back to him. Didn't you hear me?
Herbert Yes, my dear. (*He hesitates*)

The atmosphere is tense and the others are watching

But my dear, it's Christmas Day.
Alathea The time of the year is immaterial. I will not allow you to carry a flask filled with brandy.
Alec For Pete's sake, why not?
Alathea I was not addressing myself to you!

Alec I suppose you're afraid he might stand up to you one day if he gets a couple of drinks inside him.
Alathea Don't be impertinent! (*To Herbert*) Do as I say.
Gripe Well, I've known some old crabs in my time but really ...
Alathea How dare you!
Alec If Herbert can't stand up for himself it's time somebody did it for him.
Alathea This is insufferable. (*To Herbert*) I suppose you're content to sit and do nothing as usual while I'm insulted!
Herbert (*quietly, without looking at her*) Alathea, my dear, I ...
Alathea If you were a man you wouldn't let me be subjected to such indignity.
Herbert (*wearily*) After all, my dear ...
Alathea I know better than to expect any support from you.
Herbert Shall we discuss it later, my dear, when we're alone?
Alathea Oh no! We'll have this out in front of everybody.
Belinda Oh, Mother, don't make a scene now.
Alathea I know you're all against me but it's time you realised what I've had to put up with all through my married life.
Gosforth Mrs Budgett, I'm sure we have no wish to intrude upon your ...
Alathea Selfish. That's what you've been. You never gave a thought to me or to our daughter.
Belinda Steady on, Mother. That's not true. Don't get so excited.
Alathea (*hysterically*) I am not getting excited!
Herbert My dear, if only you would ...
Alathea I've given you the best years of my life. I've devoted myself to the task of pushing you forward and never a word of thanks have I had.
Belinda Mother please! Leave Daddy alone.
Alathea That's right! You take his part against me! (*She collapses on to the settee, drumming her heels in hysteria*)
Alec Suffering cats!
Bunny Oh dear, isn't this dreadful! Can't somebody stop her?
Alathea I've sacrificed myself for you, year after year, while you sulked and fiddled with your foreign stamps! You couldn't be trusted to do a single thing yourself. Always I had to be there to guide you in the way that you should go. I despise you! You've been a burden I've had to carry all this time!
Bunny You know, I don't think it's very nice of you to speak to Mr Budgett like that.
Alathea (*turning on Bunny*) What did you say!
Bunny After all, Mr Budgett's a very kind gentleman and since you're his wife you're not being very nice, are you?
Alathea Don't speak to me, you vulgar chorus girl! You're nothing but a cheap little tart!
Herbert (*in a voice like thunder*) BE QUIET WOMAN!!!!

There is an astonished dead silence on a motionless stage

Alathea I ...

Act III

Herbert (*slamming his book down on the table with tremendous force*) SILENCE!!!!

In majestic silence Herbert rises

(*Quietly, but with a steely look in his eyes*) Wife of my bosom. Light of my life. For twenty-six years I have sat and listened to the sound of your voice. For more than a quarter of a century I have turned the other cheek while you have overruled my wishes and ordered my life, not silently, never tactfully, but with a ceaseless flow of critical comment.

Alathea Herbert, you've been drinking!
Herbert Not yet, my love, but the night is young. Mr Gripe, have you the keys of the wine cellar?
Gripe They're on me person.
Herbert Fetch me a pint of Creeching Claret.

Alathea is about to interrupt

NOT ONE WORD, WOMAN!!

Gripe exits DL

I've taken a worm's eye view long enough. The time has come for the worm to turn. I've been bullied and baited ever since my wedding night and now I'm ready for a change!
Alathea Oh Herbert, you've never spoken to me like this before.
Herbert When we married you promised to love and to cherish. Perhaps in your own way you did love me once but it is many years since last you cherished or attempted to understand me. It isn't too late to start afresh and you're not too old to try to be once more the woman I fell in love with a long, long time ago.
Alathea Herbert, I...
Herbert Don't interrupt! A better wife than you once said: "A woman moved is like a fountain troubled... muddy, ill-seeming, thick, bereft of beauty." How true that is. I want my wife to be a companion, a comforter, someone in whose esteem I can be happy... tolerant of my faults and appreciative of my qualities. From this day forward you will cease to be a dissatisifed, brawling, intolerant termagent of a woman. You will instead endeavour to be what a wife should be... loving, kind, warmhearted, helpful and gracious. Is that too much to ask? You will greet me with a friendly smile and if you cannot share my interests you will at least respect them. Do I make myself clear?
Alathea Oh... Herbert! (*She collapses into her handkerchief*)

Belinda comes forward, puts her arms about her father's neck and kisses him

Belinda (*simply*) Daddy, darling, I love you.
Alec Congratulations old boy. I didn't know you had it in you.
Herbert (*sotto voce*) Quite frankly, neither did I.

Gripe enters DL *with a pint tankard*

Gosforth (*in awe*) May I shake you by the hand, sir?

Gripe 'Ere you are, sir. The warrior's reward.
Bunny (*her eyes shining*) I hope you'll be very happy.

She kisses Herbert's cheek and turns to move away, but he stops her, holding her hand

Herbert I am happy. Shall I tell you why? It's because you won't have to go back to the circus.
Bunny But ...
Herbert I'm going to open a bookshop here in the village. I want you to help me. Will you be my assistant?
Lydia That's a splendid idea!
Herbert Would you like that?
Bunny Oh! It would be wonderful!
Alec (*opening the door of the drinks cabinet*) This calls for a celebration.
Bunny I don't know if I'll be any good at it but I'll try ever so hard.
Herbert Thank you, Bunny. (*He smiles and squeezes her hand*) Thank you.
Lydia (*picking up Herbert's book from the table*) So this is what you've been reading?
Belinda What is it? ... Oh, Daddy ... *The Taming of the Shrew*. (*She links her arm in his*)
Herbert Put it back in the bookcase. I shan't need it again.

Alec has found the drinks cabinet depleted

Alec (*to Gripe*) Fetch another bottle of whisky, will you?
Gripe (*grinning*) Right you are sir.

Gripe exits DL

Cyril Just you be your charming self and the customers will come from miles around.

Cyril produces a sprig of mistletoe from behind his back, holds it over Bunny's head and kisses her. An air of relaxed gaiety has followed the tension of the previous scene. There is general laughter

Alec Now me! Now me! (*He takes the mistletoe from Cyril and follows his example*) With Bunny in the bookshop success is assured.

Alathea has risen, still sniffling. She takes the mistletoe from Alec and holds it pathetically over Herbert's head

Alathea Oh, Herbert. (*She kisses his cheek*)
Herbert (*patting her hand*) It's all right, my dear.
Alec Three cheers for Herbert Budgett! Hip ... Hip ...

There are cheers and laughter from all, suddenly interrupted by a loud and urgent knocking at the main door. The laughter dies away

Gosforth Who can that be?

Knocking again

Alec (*to Cyril*) Well, go on. Don't just stand there.

Act III

Cyril cautiously opens the door

Emily (*in the doorway*) Where are they? Where are those blasted relatives of mine?
Cyril I'm afraid you must have the wrong address . . .
Emily (*belligerently*) Wrong address, young man! This is Creeching Cheyney, all right. Stand aside!

Emily brushes him aside with a back-handed sweep of her rolled umbrella and enters, trailing snow from her snowshoes. She is a fierce little spinster with bright beady eyes. She is very Scots

I thought as much. Vultures picking over the corpse.
Gosforth Oh! Merciful Heaven!
Alathea You!
Herbert I'm not mistaken am I? You must be . . .
Emily Budgett's the name. Same as yours. Haven't seen you for twenty years. Or your stiff-necked wife.
Alathea How dare you!
Emily Sized *you* up first time I ever saw you. You were pretty then in a stuck up way. Och, what the years can do to a woman. You've not worn well.
Alathea Why have you come here? What do you want?
Emily What do I want? I want my rights, that's what. I'll not be cut out of Desmond's will. He was no right in his head and that's a fact. I can prove it in the High Court if I have to.
Gosforth Madam . . .
Emily Who are you?
Gosforth My name is Gosforth. Mr Cheyney appointed me as his executor. By the terms of the will . . .
Emily The will's no valid. If you all think you've struck it rich you can think again. You've no got your hands on the bawbies yet!
Alathea How dare you!
Emily Did you ever know the old sinner? No, you did not. But I knew him well, as you're doubtless aware. As I remember you were always the one for poking your nose into other people's affairs.
Herbert I'll thank you to keep your opinions to yourself, Aunt Emily. Whether you like it or not, this is my house and if you're going to make insulting remarks about my wife I'll show you the door.
Alathea (*a new look in her eyes*) Oh . . . Herbert . . . Herbert . . . (*She sits again, gazing at Herbert*)
Belinda Good for you, Daddy!
Emily What's this you say?
Herbert I've no wish to see you defrauded and if Uncle Desmond hasn't made allowance for you, I think he should have done, and I'll gladly make over to you half of my own inheritance.
Emily (*amazed*) Do you mean that?
Herbert I do. There's no doubt that he treated you very shabbily all those years ago and it's only fair that you should receive compensation.
Emily I'll say this for you, you're a man, Herbert Budgett, and not at all

what I'd been expecting. I'm glad to know you and I see no reason why we shouldna be friends. Here's my hand on it.

They shake hands

Och, there's no sense in holding a grudge against you for what Uncle Desmond did. He's dead and gone and that's the end of him. If he knew what a low opinion I had of him I daresay he'd rise from his grave.

Gripe enters with a bottle of whisky and a tray. He is no longer dressed as Santa Claus

Gripe Who's for a nice drop of Scotch?

Emily freezes at the sound of his voice, turns, sees him, screams and falls in a dead faint on the floor. Gripe drops the tray. All except Gripe and Gosforth flock to Emily, in concern. Ad lib consternation

(*Addressing Gosforth across the stage*) What's she doing here?

But Gosforth can only clear his throat in reply

(*Suddenly convulsed with laughter*) Here, wait a minute, let me get at her.

Gripe pushes his way through to Emily, who is moaning on the floor. She is sitting supported against Alec's knee, Herbert is offering her the brandy flask, the others are chafing her hands, etc. They look at Gripe in astonishment

I haven't laughed so much for years! Oh dear, oh dear, oh dear!

Gripe flaps his table napkin at Emily. After a moment she opens her eyes

Alec She's coming round.

Emily sees Gripe's grinning face and screams again

Emily Go away! You're dead!

Gripe goes off into paroxysms again

Gripe Oh no, I ain't.
Bunny It's all right. It's only Gripe.
Emily You mean he's alive?

Gripe convulses again, and wipes his streaming eyes

Yes, I can see you are. But I read it in the newspapers. Oh, you wicked old scoundrel! What have you been up to?
Cyril What's all this about?
Belinda Did you know Gripe before?
Alec Is he a friend of yours?
Emily Gripe? What's Gripe? This wicked old sinner's no a friend of mine, I'm telling you. Not after the way he left me waiting like a fool at the kirk of St Andrew's.
Alathea Who did?
Emily (*pointing at Gripe*) He did! ... Your Uncle Desmond!

Act III

Alathea ⎫ ⎧ What!
Alec ⎬ (*together*) ⎨ Who?
Cyril ⎭ ⎩ Him?
Herbert You mean that *he* is Uncle Desmond Cheyney?
Bunny Well, I never!
Belinda Rich Uncle Desmond who's left us all his money?
Alathea Are you sure?
Emily Sure? Of course I'm sure! Look at him, the old devil, having the time of his life, laughing at us, every one of us!
Gripe Ho! Ho! Ho! . . . He! He! He!
Emily I'm glad you find it so funny.
Gripe (*helpless with laughter*) If you could have seen the look on your face . . . You're all looking very surprised . . . Ho! Ho! Ho! . . . You've all got your mouths open.

Seven pairs of jaws close simultaneously

Belinda (*observing Gosforth, who is still standing apart from the others over right*) I notice he's not looking surprised. Were you in on this?
Gosforth (*chuckling*) Well, as a matter of fact . . .
Herbert As a matter of fact you two have been making fools of the lot of us. Is that it?
Gosforth No, no. Not really. The legacies are genuine enough. Isn't that so, Mr Cheyney?
Gripe Oh yes, that's quite right. I promise you won't be out of pocket just because Emily's upset the apple cart. You'll get the money just the same. The only difference is you'll get it while I'm alive. You won't have to wait till I'm dead.
Emily That's all very well, but what about me?
Gripe You're an enterprising woman, Emily. I'd not counted on you turning up. There's not many women would have come through snow and ice on a day like this. (*He eyes her with admiration*)
Alec How did you manage to get here? I thought the roads were all covered over.
Emily So they are. I've been four days coming down from Scotland in my little Austin Seven with chains round the wheels . . .

The ghostly chains of Act One are heard rattling again far off. Everybody listens

What was that?
Cyril The plumbing I expect.
Emily And I've done the last lap on foot as you can see.
Gripe 'Ere, come 'ere. Come and sit down.

Gripe makes Emily sit on the settee and starts to unlace her snowshoes

Let's get these tennis racquets off you. (*He chuckles*) What a girl. You don't half look silly.
Emily Is that so? Well, let me tell you, Desmond Cheyney . . .

Gripe Wait a minute, Emily. Before you start, I want to tell you something. You may not believe me but I'm sorry for what I did. The fact is I've always had a horror of getting wed. I've been such a lad in my time that the thought of marriage seemed rather abnormal. I couldn't go through with it. But I've often regretted it and now I'm going to ask you something.
Emily Don't tell me you're going to pop the question again?
Gripe Well, why not? Anyway, it was you who popped it last time.
Emily May God forgive you for a lying old ...
Gripe (*chuckling*) Go on, you tried to sweep me off me feet, you know you did. But I wouldn't be swept.
Emily Well, I like that!
Gripe I've tried everything once and I've run out of original sins so I think I'll have a go at matrimony as a last resort. Now's the time, while we're still young.
Emily You're a sinful and wicked old man, Desmond Cheyney, but I've always had a soft spot for you. All right, I'll have you. But this time you'll put it in writing!
Gripe (*winking at the others*) I always was a success with the girls.
Alec What a family I'm marrying into!
Herbert What's that?
Belinda Oh yes, I knew there was something I forgot to tell you. Alec and I are engaged.
Lydia What an odd coincidence. Cyril accepted me in the kitchen.
Gripe It spreads like a contagion, don't it?
Alathea Well, I must say ...
Herbert Quiet Alathea.
Alathea Yes, dear.
Herbert Where's my nightcap?
Gripe Here you are sir.

Gripe hands Herbert the tankard from the table. He then proceeds to pour out whiskies for all, including Alathea, with Alec's assistance

Herbert I'm beginning to realize the terms of your will weren't really as eccentric as they seemed! In fact there was sound sense behind them.
Belinda There certainly was. (*She hugs Alec's arm affectionately*)
Herbert On behalf of us all I want to tell Uncle Desmond how much we appreciate the very original Christmas he has given us at Creeching Cheyney. It's done us all a lot of good. Here's your very good health and that of all the other recently engaged persons in this house. Not forgetting you, Aunt Emily. May you have many merry Christmasses to come. I give you a toast to our host. (*Raising his glass*) Uncle Desmond!
All Uncle Desmond! (*They drink*)
Alec Speech!
All Yes, come on, Uncle Desmond. Speech!
Gripe I'm very touched ... No I don't mean up here ... (*tapping his head*) ... I mean down here (*putting his hand on his heart*). It's very nice of you

Act III

not to be angry with me. (*He starts to chuckle again*) Especially after the way I put the wind up you last night.

Lydia The ghost!

Belinda Then it was you?

Cyril But how did you do it? You came in yourself just afterwards from down there.

Gripe You don't think it was me up there doing the bogey-bogey business do you?

Herbert Who was it then?

Lydia Yes, who was it?

Gosforth clears his throat. All look towards him

Gosforth (*with a giggle*) I cannot tell a lie. It was I. (*He lifts his arms in ghostly fashion and makes a haunting noise. Then he starts to laugh*)

Gripe He's been having a wonderful time. I don't know how he's kept a straight face, honest I don't.

Gosforth (*almost crying with unaccustomed laughter*) I thought I should have died!

Alec (*laughing*) Well, I'm damned! You mean this house isn't really haunted after all?

At this Gripe and Gosforth howl with laughter and weep on each other's shoulders

Gripe No. It was just a joke to see whether they'd rather be frightened to death than lose all that lovely money.

Cyril (*laughing*) Well, I'm blowed. So there are no ghosts here at all.

By now everybody is laughing

Gripe No! . . . Not even a teeny-weeny one!

This is greeted with a fresh outburst of helpless mirth from everybody. Almost immediately the lights go out and there is a violent clanking of chains. Horrifying screams, ghostly whisperings and sobbing noises are heard through an amplifier. Lightning. Thunder and gusts of wind are heard

The kitchen door opens by itself, as in Act Two, and a terrifying shadow with arms raised falls across the stage

Green spots shine on to the panic-stricken faces of Gripe and the rest

A luminous skeleton dangles from the ceiling. A figure with a white face leans out from the panel UC

The ghost of Montague Cheyney stalks down the stairs towards its victims

Everyone makes a mad rush for the doorway, where they become wedged. the noise is deafening. Gripe is seen frantically trying to climb over the top of the scrum as the spectre reaches him . . . and——

The CURTAIN *falls*

FURNITURE AND PROPERTY LIST

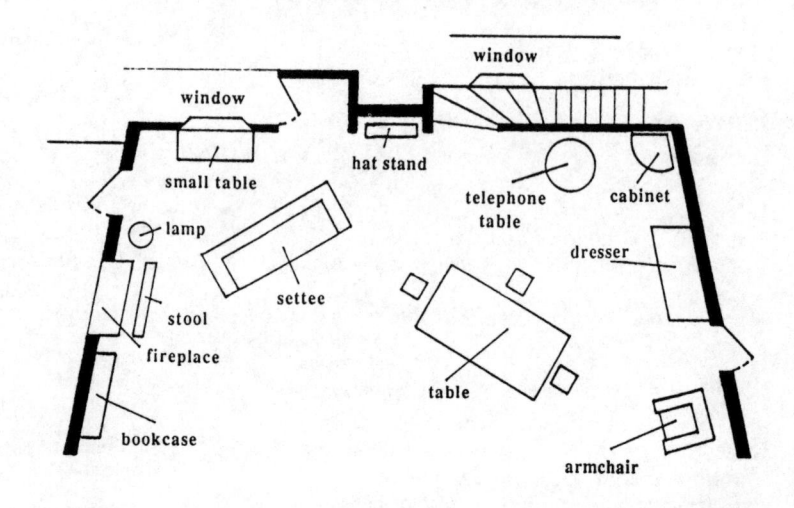

[Floor plan showing room layout with the following labels: window (top), window (upper left), small table, lamp, hat stand, telephone table, cabinet, dresser, stool, settee, fireplace, table, bookcase, armchair]

ACT I

On stage: Dining table
Settee
Armchair
Umbrella stand-cum-coat rack. *In tray:* envelope containing letter from Gosforth
Small telephone table. *On it:* telephone
Drinks cabinet
Long firestool
Three upright chairs
Standard lamp
Wall brackets
Small table in front of window
Sundry bookcases. One containing a dozen or more old books with identical bindings (Shakespeare)
Stags heads, halberds at producer's discretion
Heavy curtains for large window
Large faded carpet
Four large white sheets covering furniture
Dressing at producer's discretion

Laughter in the Dark

Off stage: Two large suitcases **(Herbert)**
Small suitcase. *In it:* towels, sponge bag etc **(Belinda)**
Suitcase **(Cyril)**
Small Christmas tree **(Alec)**
Two carrier bags. *In them:* gaily wrapped parcels, goose (wrapped), bottle of whisky, bottle of champagne etc **(Alec)**
Long loaf of bread **(Gripe)**
String of black puddings **(Gripe)**
Tray containing three plates and tablecloth **(Gripe)**
Hunk of cheese **(Gripe)**
Log for fire **(Gripe)**
Moth-eaten dirty green baize apron **(Herbert)**
Knives and forks **(Gripe)**
Four soup plates **(Gripe)**
Football rattle **(Gripe)**
Large soup tureen and lid **(Gripe)**
Two dead mice **(Gripe)**

Personal: **Gripe:** matches
Thundercloud: tomahawk
Alec: two large cigars

ACT II

Strike: All props except permanent ones

Set: Logs by fire
Alec's, Cyril's and Herbert's overcoats on coat rack
Check Alec's overcoat contains cigar case and cigars
Check Cyril's overcoat contains cigarette case and lighter
Travelling rug on coat rack
Gosforth's bowler hat and umbrella on coat rack
Six glasses of whisky
One empty glass
Four cigars
Table napkins in rings, dishes of fruit, bowl of walnuts, pair of nutcrackers on dining table
Sundry glasses and bottles, including a depleted port bottle and a partially consumed bottle of whisky on top and insides of drinks cabinet
Belinda's suitcase near umbrella stand
Alec's suitcase containing a hot watter bottle near C door
Corkscrew in fruit dish

Off stage: Small silver tray **(Gripe)**
Pint pewter tankard containing Creeching Claret **(Gripe)**
Three bottles of Creeching Claret covered with cobwebs **(Cyril)**
Two dark coloured tumblers **(Alec)**
Branched candlestick with candles **(Gripe)**
Second bowler hat (replica of Gosforth's) with arrow attached **(Stage Management)**
Large bow and quiver of arrows **(Thundercloud)**
Bottle of champagne **(Alec)**

Personal: Pince-nez **(Gosforth)**
Sealed legal-looking document on stiff paper **(Gosforth)**
Seedy napkin **(Gripe)**
Watch—waistcoat pocket type **(Gosforth)**
Cigar cutter **(Alec)**
Pair of long black gloves, long silver dagger, silver strangling cord **(Panel spectre)**

ACT III

Strike: Suitcases
Used glasses

Re-set: Settee in original position
Move all bottles to drinks cabinet

On stage: Christmas decorations and foliage
Detachable sprig of mistletoe for Cyril
Decorated Christmas Tree
Portable radio on large table
Snow round window frames
Cyril's coat on coat stand
Gosforth's overcoat on coat stand
Handkerchief in Gosforth's coat
Nine clean glasses on top of drinks cabinet

Off stage: Spade **(Lydia)**
Chopper **(Cyril)**
Muffin bell **(Gripe)**
Large sack with eight wrapped packages, viz:
    Silver brandy flask
    Filmy négligée (white)
    Filmy négligée (black)
    Pipe
    Lighter
    Box of handkerchiefs
    Box of cigars
    Box of chocolates
Two blankets **(Lydia)**
Two blankets, one pillow **(Bunny)**
Two blankets, one pillow **(Belinda)**
Pint pewter tankard of Creeching Claret **(Gripe)**
Full bottle of whisky, silver tray, seedy napkin **(Gripe)**

Personal: **Alec:** bright paper hat, cigarette and matches, typewritten document, fountain pen
Cyril: bright paper hat
Gripe: notebook and pencil
Emily: rolled umbrella
Alathea: handkerchief

LIGHTING PLOT

One interior setting. Practical fittings required: wall lights, standard lamp

ACT I

To open: Darkness

Cue 1	**When ready** *Flash of lightning*	(Page 1)
Cue 2	**Gripe** appears with lantern *Spot to cover lantern*	(Page 1)
Cue 3	**Gripe** switches on wall lights *Bring up main lighting*	(Page 2)
Cue 4	**Alathea** switches on standard lamp *Bring up spot to cover*	(Page 3)
Cue 5	**Gripe** lights fire *Slowly bring up fire-glow*	(Page 4)

ACT II, SCENE 1

To open: All wall brackets and standard lamp on. Fire lit

No cues

ACT II, SCENE 2

To open: Moonlight, flickering firelight

Cue 6	**Alec** switches on lights *Snap up main lighting*	(Page 33)
Cue 7	As ghost of Montague Cheyney enters *Fade general lighting to emphasize ghost*	(Page 33)
Cue 8	**Herbert:** "... in the house now!" *All lights go out except for fire and moonlight*	(Page 41)
Cue 9	As apparition appears *Green spot on apparition*	(Page 41)
Cue 10	As **Gripe** enters from kitchen *Spot to cover candlelight*	(Page 41)

ACT II

To open: All practicals on. Fire lit

Cue 11	Helpless laughter from everyone *All lights go out including fire and moonlight. Lightning*	(Page 61)
Cue 12	As kitchen door opens *Green spots on cast*	(Page 61)

EFFECTS PLOT

ACT I

Cue 1	As CURTAIN rises *Rain, thunder, gusts of wind—continue. Peal of maniacal laughter. More thunder*	(Page 1)
Cue 2	**Gripe:** "Did someone knock?" *Wind howls. High pitched moaning*	(Page 1)
Cue 3	**Gripe** howls *Increase wind*	(Page 1)
Cue 4	**Gripe:** "Nobody would." *Wind rises*	(Page 2)
Cue 5	**Gripe** lights fire *Snapping, crackling from fire*	(Page 4)
Cue 6	**Belinda:** "... scare away the bats." *Telephone rings*	(Page 8)

ACT II

Cue 7	**Bunny** exits upstairs *Church bells, muffled*	(Page 31)
Cue 8	**Gripe:** "... muck heap in the snow." *Bells stop*	(Page 32)
Cue 9	**Alec:** "Old Granny Gripe's brew?" *Bells begin again. Fade when ready*	(Page 32)
Cue 10	As CURTAIN rises at beginning of SCENE 2 *Grandfather clock chimes one. Ghostly rattling of chains. Peal of mad laughter*	(Page 33)
Cue 11	**Cyril** exits *Twang of bowstring*	(Page 40)

ACT III

Cue 12	As CURTAIN rises *Choir sings "God Rest Ye Merry Gentlemen" followed by radio announcement as per script*	(Page 42)
Cue 13	**Radio announcer:** "Snow continues to fall..." *Wind howls*	(Page 42)

Cue 14	**Alec** switches off radio *Cut radio*	(Page 42)
Cue 15	**Emily:** Austin Seven with chains round the wheels." *Ghostly chains rattle*	(Page 59)
Cue 16	As Lights black out *Clanking chains, screams, whispering, sobbing. Thunder and gusts of wind*	(Page 61)

Incidental and Curtain music

This should suggest both the eerie and the comic, the effect being "spooky-comical" rather than merely weird.

A licence issued by Samuel French Ltd to perform this play does not include permission to use any Overture or Incidental music specified in this copy. Where the place of performance is already licensed by the Performing Right Society a return of the music used must be made to them. If the place of performance is not so licensed then application should be made to the PERFORMING RIGHT SOCIETY, 29 Berners Street, London W1.

A separate and additional licence from PHONOGRAPHIC PERFORMANCES LTD, Ganton House, Ganton Street, London W1, is needed whenever commercial recordings are used.